TAKE A WALK IN THEIR SHOES

Imagine yourself walking in the footsteps of these African-Americans—fourteen courageous people who made a difference:

Martin Luther King, Jr.
Rosa Parks
Arthur A. Schomburg
Leontyne Price
Charles White
Garrett A. Morgan
Daniel "Chappie" James
Charles Drew
Frederick Douglass
Ida B. Wells
Oscar Micheaux
Mary McLeod Bethune
Leroy "Satchel" Paige
Maggie Lena Walker

To Alex from Moms' Dad ♥ 2/14/93

TAKE A WALK IN THEIR SHOES

Glennette Tilley Turner

ILLUSTRATED BY

Elton C. Fax

Puffin Books

PUFFIN BOOKS
Published by the Penguin Group
Penguin Books USA Inc., 375 Hudson Street, New York, New York 10014, U.S.A.
Penguin Books Ltd, 27 Wrights Lane, London W8 5TZ, England
Penguin Books Australia Ltd, Ringwood, Victoria, Australia
Penguin Books Canada Ltd, 10 Alcorn Avenue, Toronto, Ontario, Canada M4V 3B2
Penguin Books (N.Z.) Ltd, 182–190 Wairau Road, Auckland 10, New Zealand

Penguin Books Ltd, Registered Offices: Harmondsworth, Middlesex, England

First published in the United States of America by E.P. Dutton,
a division of Penguin Books USA Inc., 1989
Published in Puffin Books, 1992

1   3   5   7   9   10   8   6   4   2

LIBRARY OF CONGRESS CATALOGING-IN-PUBLICATION DATA
Turner, Glennette Tilley.
Take a walk in their shoes / by Glennette Tilley Turner;
illustrated by Elton C. Fax.   p. cm.
Originally published: New York: Cobblehill Books, 1989.
Includes index.
Summary: Presents biographical sketches of Fourteen notable
African-Americans, including Martin Luther King, Jr., Rosa Parks,
and "Satchel" Paige, accompanied by brief skits in which readers can
act out imagined scenes from their lives.
ISBN 0-14-036250-9
1. Afro-Americans—Biography—Juvenile literature. [1. Afro-
Americans—Biography. 2. Afro-Americans—Drama. 3. Plays.]
I. Fax, Elton C., ill. II. Title.
E185.96.T85 1992   920'.009296073—dc20   [B]   [920]   92-19524

Printed in the United States of America
Set in Palatino

To my parents,
John Lee Tilley and Phyllis Jones Tilley,
for being my role models
and to
"Spike" Middleton Harris,
a tireless researcher
of African-American history

❧

Contents

Introduction   ix

MARTIN LUTHER KING, JR.   13
   In the Footsteps of Dr. King   20

ROSA PARKS   25
   The Unexpected Heroine   31

ARTHUR A. SCHOMBURG   35
   A Legacy of Dignity and Pride   42

LEONTYNE PRICE   49
   The Priceless Leontyne   54

CHARLES WHITE   59
   A Turning Point in the Life
   of Charles White   63

GARRETT A. MORGAN   69
   Meet the Inventor of the Stoplight   76

DANIEL "CHAPPIE" JAMES   81
   "The Eagles Return to the Nest"   88

CHARLES DREW   92
    Who Was Dr. Charles Drew?   98

FREDERICK DOUGLASS   105
    The Douglass "Station"
    of the Underground Railroad   110

IDA B. WELLS   115
    The Beauty of Being Free   122

OSCAR MICHEAUX   129
    Oscar Micheaux's Visit   134

MARY McLEOD BETHUNE   139
    Let Them Have Schools   145

LEROY "SATCHEL" PAIGE   149
    The Rediscovery of "Satchel" Paige   156

MAGGIE LENA WALKER   161
    Miracles Do Happen!   166

INDEX   171

Introduction

IMAGINE YOURSELF walking in the footsteps of:

MARTIN LUTHER KING, JR., the civil rights leader who made such an impact on the twentieth century that we commemorate his birth with a national holiday

ROSA PARKS, the seamstress who politely refused to give up her bus seat and changed the course of history

ARTHUR ALFONSO SCHOMBURG, the book lover who found the missing pages in black history and left this legacy to present and future generations

MARY MCLEOD BETHUNE, an educator who was so determined to open a much-needed school that she started with just $1.50

IDA B. WELLS, a former teacher who educated readers with the newspaper articles she wrote

FREDERICK DOUGLASS, a magnificent speaker and writer who had been punished as a slave for trying to learn to read and write

LEONTYNE PRICE, who has thrilled music lovers with the magnificence of her voice

CHARLES WHITE, an artist who expressed his genius by painting images of dignity

OSCAR MICHEAUX, a supersalesman who pioneered in the art of film making

"SATCHEL" PAIGE, the baseball legend who turned pitching into an art form

MAGGIE LENA WALKER, the banker who understood that little bits of money can add up to a lot

CHARLES DREW whose contributions in the field of medicine have saved the lives of many injured people

GARRETT A. MORGAN whose invention of the electric stoplight has prevented numerous traffic injuries from occurring

DANIEL "CHAPPIE" JAMES, the flying ace who became America's first black four-star general

Pretend to be them. Read their life stories. Act out their skits. (Since we were not actually there, we can't know exactly what they said, but these skits attempt to capture the essence of what these great people thought and did.) You can read more books on their lives to get even better acquainted with them. Use your own imagination to make the skits as simple or as elaborate as you wish.

You will experience the feeling of turning back the pages of history and walking in the footsteps of these African-American achievers. When you realize how they succeeded against all odds, you will see new possibilities for realizing your own dreams.

TAKE A WALK
IN THEIR SHOES

MARTIN LUTHER KING, JR.

DR. MARTIN LUTHER KING, JR., was such a great man that we have a national holiday to celebrate his birthday. He believed in a world where there would be no discrimination or prejudice or violence. He spent his life working not only for blacks but for all people. He wanted civil rights and justice for all. "Everybody is somebody," he said. He believed that every person deserves to be treated fairly.

Martin Luther King, Jr., was born in Atlanta, Georgia, on January 15, 1929. He was the oldest son of the Reverend and Mrs. Martin Luther King. He was named Michael Luther after his father, but later the Reverend King changed both their names to Martin Luther in honor of the great church leader.

Martin's father was pastor of the Ebenezer Baptist Church in Atlanta. His mother, Alberta Williams King, had been a schoolteacher. On Sundays she directed the church choir and played the organ for services. Martin's sister, Christine, was a year older than he was. His brother, Alfred Daniel, was a year younger.

The King family lived with the "Jim Crow" laws that existed at that time in Atlanta and throughout the South. These laws tried to keep blacks and whites separated. Drinking fountains, buses, bathrooms, almost everything was segregated. Too often there were signs that said, "Whites Only." And the accommodations for black people were usually far less desirable than those for whites.

Unhappy racial experiences made a deep and lasting impression on young Martin. One day his father took him to buy new shoes. When they sat down in the store, the clerk asked them to move to the back of the store. Dr. King said that they were comfortably seated. The clerk refused to wait on them if they wouldn't move. Dr. King took Martin by the hand and left the store rather than take that kind of treatment. Another time, the parents of boys Martin played with told him that they could no longer come out to play with him because they were white and he was black. Martin's feelings were hurt. His mother tried to explain about prejudice. She told him that blacks were no longer slaves, but they were not really free. Martin Luther King, Jr., would remember that and would try to do something about it.

Martin liked sports. He played baseball and basketball. Wrestling was another one of his favorite sports. He had other interests, too. He especially loved to read. He liked reading about famous people in black history. He found out what it took for them to overcome difficulties and become successful. He liked to learn new words and use them. When he got to high school, his ability to use words enabled him to win an oratorical contest. Listening to his father's sermons made him realize the power of words. If you could speak well, people would listen to you.

When he was only fifteen, Martin Luther King, Jr., entered Morehouse College in Atlanta. It was a black college, and his father and grandfather had gone there. He knew that his father would like him to become a minister, but at first Martin was not sure that was what he wanted to do. After meeting and talking with Dr. Benjamin E. Mays, the college president, and Professor George Kelsey, head of the religion department, he made up his mind. At eighteen he was ordained a minister. The next year he graduated from Morehouse College.

During summers Martin worked to earn money. One summer he worked in Connecticut where there was no segregation for blacks. He got to know white workers. When he went to

study at Crozer Theological Seminary in Chester, Pennsylvania, he was in a school with white students for the first time. He began to realize that people were just people, no matter what their color.

Martin was an excellent student and was the class valedictorian when he graduated in 1951 with a Bachelor of Divinity degree from Crozer. He received a scholarship to Boston University where he could study for his doctor's degree in theology.

While at Boston University, Martin met Coretta Scott, a beautiful young music student from Marion, Alabama. She was studying voice at the New England Conservatory. She and Martin were married in June, 1953. His father performed the ceremony at her home in Alabama.

Coretta had grown up with segregation too. She shared Martin's dream of a time when everyone everywhere could enjoy equal rights. When he had completed his studies, the couple decided that they could make the greatest contribution by going back down South to work. Martin was installed by his father as pastor of the Dexter Avenue Baptist Church in Montgomery, Alabama, in October of 1954. Just a little more than a year later, Yolanda, the first of the Kings' four children, was born.

In December of 1955, Mrs. Rosa Parks refused to give up her seat on a Montgomery bus, and a bus boycott was planned. Dr. King was asked to help, as was his friend, the Reverend Ralph Abernathy. Blacks walked to work or took cars or taxis, but they did not ride the buses. Finally, after more than a year of protest—during which a bomb had been thrown into the

King home—the United States Supreme Court ruled that segregation on buses was against the law.

Martin Luther King, Jr., knew that even though that battle against bus discrimination had been won in Montgomery, there was more that needed doing. In 1957, he organized the Southern Christian Leadership Conference (SCLC) to fight "Jim Crow" laws that discriminated against blacks. Offices for the new group were in Atlanta, and the Kings moved there. Martin became assistant pastor at his father's church, the Ebenezer Baptist Church. He spent much time traveling. He spoke all over the country, urging nonviolent ways of gaining civil rights. He and Mrs. King visited Europe and Africa. They went to India to study Mahatma Gandhi's nonviolent ways of fighting for freedom.

In the early 1960s, black and white college students were attempting to end discrimination at eating places for "Whites Only" and on interstate buses. Dr. King's organization, SCLC, gave support to these efforts, which were undertaken by the Student Nonviolent Coordinating Committee and the Congress for Racial Equality. The nonviolent protests were often met with violence. The "Freedom Riders" were attacked and beaten; one of their buses was burned.

There were beatings and violence in Montgomery. When Dr. King led a freedom march in Birmingham, Alabama, he and other protestors were jailed. There were hundreds of other freedom marches. As a result, segregation of blacks and whites was ended in many places, though there was still a need to work against discrimination.

After Governor George Wallace tried to stop integration of

students at the University of Alabama, and Medgar Evers, a civil rights leader, was assassinated in Jackson, Mississippi, the biggest protest march of all was held. It was the historic March on Washington, D.C., in August of 1963. Over 200,000 people, blacks and whites, took part. Martin Luther King, Jr., spoke to them on the steps of the Lincoln Memorial. It was his famous "I Have a Dream" speech. "I have a dream that one day on the red hills of Georgia the sons of former slaves and the sons of former slave owners will be able to sit down together at the table of brotherhood," he said. He asked everyone to join hands and sing the words of an old Negro spiritual, "Free at last! Free at last!"

Dr. King and other civil rights leaders continued to work for what they knew was right. They worked to get blacks to register to vote. They worked to get equal use of public accommodations. There was violence, and Dr. King was discouraged by that. But more and more people around the world were beginning to take notice. Support for Martin Luther King, Jr., received international recognition when he was awarded the Nobel Peace Prize in 1964.

Dr. King still could not relax, however. He knew that there was still a long way to go, and he was not willing to give up his efforts to help his people. In 1966, he and his family moved to Chicago. People in the slums of big cities had problems that were as serious as the discrimination they faced in the South. King planned a Poor People's March on Washington, D.C. It would include poor blacks, whites, native Americans, Mexicans, and Puerto Ricans and present their concerns to the government.

Shortly before the march, Dr. King went to Memphis, Tennessee, where garbage workers were on strike for better working conditions. He led marchers through the streets in support of the strike. Violence broke out, and a young man was killed.

On April 4, King stood on the balcony of his motel in Memphis, talking with men who had been with him in his many civil rights efforts. Across the street, James Earl Ray took aim and fired his gun. His bullet assassinated Martin Luther King, Jr. Ray was later captured and convicted of the killing.

Martin Luther King, Jr., was only thirty-nine years old when he died. He was mourned by millions, both blacks and whites. He had brought about needed changes. He was indeed a great man. It is only right that on the third Monday of January his country celebrates the anniversary of his birth.

In the Footsteps of
Dr. King

CAST

Father   Three children:
Mother   A preschooler (age five)
                  An elementary school student
                  A junior high school student

SCENE 1

Setting: Family is gathered around the television set at home in Mont-gomery, Alabama. It is January 15, the birthday of Martin Luther King, Jr., and they have just watched an excellent TV program about Dr. King. They are sitting quietly, each person thinking about the program they've just seen.

ELEMENTARY STUDENT: Dad and Mom, were you alive when Dr. King was marching for freedom?

MOTHER: (*smiling*) Yes, we both were. We were young, but we were very much alive.

FATHER: Those were such thrilling times. I remember I marched with my parents when Dr. King came to town. We marched for the chance to use public facilities. I loved to read, so I especially wanted to be able to use the public library. Sometimes it seemed that any change was so slow. Sometimes you felt like giving up. Then you'd look around, and some changes had been made.

JUNIOR HIGH STUDENT: I wish I had been living then.

PRESCHOOLER: Me, too.

ELEMENTARY STUDENT: So do I.

FATHER: Tell you what, your mother and I realize that children today don't know as much about Martin Luther King, Jr., as we did.

MOTHER: We thought you might want to visit some of the places that were important in Dr. King's life.

FATHER: Would you like that?

ALL THREE CHILDREN: (*together*) Yes!

MOTHER: We could make it our vacation trip this year. We may have to do without some other things in order to pay for it, but we feel it is important.

FATHER: (*to children*) We can pack up and go as soon as school is out for the summer. I can arrange my vacation time then. What do you think of that?

JUNIOR HIGH STUDENT: That will be the next best thing to having lived when Martin Luther King, Jr., was alive.

ELEMENTARY STUDENT: That will be fun!

PRESCHOOLER: Oh, goodie.

MOTHER: Well, you'll have to do some homework first. Read up on the places that were important to Dr. King and what he did there, so you'll know what you would like to see. Then we'll talk about this later and you'll be able to say where you would like to go.

FATHER: You can be the tour guides.

SCENE 2

Setting: At the dinner table on April 4, the anniversary of the assassination of Dr. King. The family has just seen another TV program about Martin Luther King, Jr.,'s life. This time, the children were eager to start talking as soon as the program ended.

JUNIOR HIGH STUDENT: Mom, Dad, we've been gathering information for our Martin Luther King, Jr., trip.

FATHER: I'm glad you've taken such an interest.

ELEMENTARY STUDENT: Well, these are some places that were important to Dr. King. Montgomery is one of them.

JUNIOR HIGH STUDENT: The civil rights movement got started right here in Montgomery.

FATHER: It sure did. This is where Rosa Parks refused to give up her seat on a bus and the bus boycott was held.

ELEMENTARY STUDENT: Birmingham and Selma are other places where Dr. King led freedom marches. They are right here in Alabama, too.

JUNIOR HIGH STUDENT: Dr. King wasn't afraid of anything. His house got bombed one time. And he went to jail another time. Do you suppose we could see some of the places where they had freedom marches? I'd like that.

MOTHER: My goodness, you really have read up on things.

FATHER: It seems to me that we could certainly visit the places here in Alabama and then get to Atlanta. That's where Dr. King was born and where his father had his church.

ELEMENTARY STUDENT: That's right. Atlanta is on our list. And there's Washington, D.C. Martin Luther King, Jr., led the March on Washington.

JUNIOR HIGH STUDENT: I'd really like to have heard him there. They had 200,000 people. Dad, did you and Mom get to go?

FATHER: No, but we saw it all on television. It was really inspiring.

ELEMENTARY STUDENT: That's when he said, "I have a dream."

PRESCHOOLER: Are we going to Washington?

MOTHER: Well, I don't think we can travel that far this summer. But there's lots to see and find out about right close to home.

ELEMENTARY STUDENT: Hey, this is fun! Can we get a map and plan out the best way to go?

FATHER: That's a good idea.

MOTHER: You can work out the best route and what the mileage will be.

PRESCHOOLER: I bet I can find places on a map.

JUNIOR HIGH STUDENT: I'm going to like this. I'll be the navigator.

ELEMENTARY STUDENT: (*to Junior High Student*) I'm better at figuring out the mileage. You won't get it added up right.

JUNIOR HIGH STUDENT: Who says so? But you do it if you want to. I'll still be the navigator and say where we go next.

MOTHER: (*laughing*) It will take all of us to get things planned carefully.

FATHER: Well, you kids are off to a good start. I'm just glad you care enough about Martin Luther King, Jr., to want to do this. Maybe you will understand better just what King meant to this country.

ROSA PARKS

Most historians agree that the civil rights movement was born in one fateful moment. That was the moment when Rosa Parks, a seamstress in a Montgomery, Alabama, department store, decided that she was tired of racial segregation and refused to give up her bus seat to someone who got on the bus after she did. Because of this action and the efforts to gain equal rights which followed it, Rosa Parks became known as "the mother of the civil rights movement."

Rosa Parks' early life gave no hint that she was destined to do something that would eventually change the course of history. When she was a little girl growing up in Tuskegee, Alabama, no one could have guessed that she would become "the mother of the civil rights movement." Born on February 4, 1913, she was the daughter of a carpenter and a former schoolteacher. She attended public school in her hometown. Later, she took courses at Alabama State College for Negroes in nearby Montgomery.

Rosa met and married Raymond A. Parks. They made their home in Montgomery. Mr. Parks was a barber. Mrs. Parks had done clerical work and been an insurance saleswoman. However, she was working as a tailor's assistant at a department store on the day when she made history.

Rosa Parks wasn't a person to seek fame. Instead, she was a soft-spoken, mild-mannered, hardworking lady. She was also a caring person and, in her quiet way, a very courageous one.

She was the secretary and youth adviser for the local chapter of the National Association for the Advancement of Colored People, and she worked with the Voters League to register black people to vote. This community work was dangerous in those days because of local laws and feelings. Mrs. Parks believed that everyone—both blacks and whites—should have the rights and responsibilities of citizenship, and she did what she could to help make this possible.

Then came December 1, 1955.

At that time, the city buses had a small section in the back that was reserved for black people. The rest of the space was reserved for white people.

On that particular day, Rosa Parks got on the bus after a hard day's work. She sat in the first seat behind the section reserved for white passengers. That reserved section was not filled at the time she boarded the bus. A couple of stops later a number of white passengers got on. All but one found seats in the section for whites. The bus driver ordered Mrs. Parks and three other black passengers to give up their seats. All the other seats on the bus were now filled, so if Rosa Parks had moved, she would have had to stand. She had paid her fare and was comfortably seated, so she politely refused to give up her seat. She did this, knowing that this particular bus driver

would be unkind. Twelve years earlier, Mrs. Parks had had an unpleasant encounter with him.

She was not surprised that the bus driver called the police to arrest her. Two policemen came. They escorted Rosa Parks to the police car, then went back to the bus to ask the driver if he wanted to swear out a warrant. He did.

Rosa Parks was taken to jail and fingerprinted. A date was set for her to go to court. She telephoned Mr. E. D. Nixon, head of the Progressive Democrats and former president of the state and local NAACP. He signed her bail—that is, he put up money so she would not have to stay in jail until her day in court. At first, Mr. Nixon and very few other people knew of the arrest.

The next morning, Mr. Nixon called Dr. Martin Luther King, Jr.—a young minister who had recently come to Montgomery—to tell him about it. For more than fifty years "Jim Crow" laws had been in effect in southern states. This meant that black and white citizens were expected to sit in separate places on buses, on trains, and in movie theaters. There were separate drinking fountains and rest rooms. Most often the space provided for black citizens was smaller and less comfortable than that provided for white citizens. Black citizens had been unhappy about this unequal treatment. Over the years they had shown their displeasure whenever possible, but there had not been a unified effort to end "Jim Crow" practices.

Mr. Nixon felt that the time had come to boycott the buses instead of taking this kind of indignity any longer. He suggested a meeting of ministers and civic leaders to talk about the matter.

Before calling Dr. King, Mr. Nixon had called the Reverend Ralph Abernathy who, like Dr. King, was a young minister in Montgomery. The three men worked out plans for the meeting.

Many people attended. It was agreed that there would be a bus boycott beginning Monday, December 5. Dr. King was chosen to lead the boycott.

Leaflets and telephone calls spread the word. One of the leaflets was handed to a maid who couldn't read very well. She gave it to her employer. The employer quickly called the newspaper. Instead of working against the boycott, an article in the newspaper helped spread the word to more people.

For the next year, black people in Montgomery refused to ride the buses. They walked, they rode bicycles, they shared car pools, they took taxis to work. The boycott was effective because black riders made up 65 percent of the bus company's customers and they were no longer riding the buses.

During the boycott, Dr. King and other leaders held meetings to encourage the people to continue not using the buses. Many white people tried to stop the boycott. Many black people who had done nothing wrong were arrested. One night someone threw a bomb into the King home. Dr. King, who had been at a meeting, rushed home to find out if Coretta and the baby were safe. They were all right.

Court cases were brought to get the "Jim Crow" laws changed. The cases went all the way to the United States Supreme Court. Finally, the Supreme Court ruled that bus segregation was illegal. No longer could blacks in Montgomery be forced to sit in the back on buses or to give up their seats for white passengers.

Thanks to Rosa Parks' courageous action and the many Montgomery citizens who worked together, the buses were desegregated. Every bus customer could take a seat on a first-come, first-served basis. It was the beginning of the civil rights movement. Dr. Martin Luther King, Jr., would be in the spotlight as one of its leaders. And Rosa Parks would be remembered for her part in changing history.

The Unexpected Heroine

શ્

CAST

Narrator	Passengers on bus
Rosa Parks	First policeman
First woman	Second policeman
Another bystander	Mr. E. D. Nixon
Bus driver	

SCENE 1

NARRATOR: Some historical turning points start out uneventfully. Such is the story of Mrs. Rosa Parks.

FIRST WOMAN: (*approaching bus stop*) Hello, Rosa. How are you?

ROSA PARKS: All right. How are you?

FIRST WOMAN: Fine—just tired after a hard day's work.

ANOTHER BYSTANDER: I hope we can get a seat. It's a shame—the few seats they have for colored people on the bus.

ROSA PARKS: It sure is. Here comes the bus.

NARRATOR: The bus pulls up and the three women get on and pay their fares.

FIRST WOMAN: Just like I thought. There are not many seats left for us. Rosa, you take this one. I'll get one farther back.

ROSA PARKS: Thank you.

NARRATOR: Rosa Parks had just started to relax when the bus stopped again and several white passengers got on. Most of the new passengers found seats, but one man was left standing. The bus driver noticed that man and called to Rosa Parks and three other black people sitting beside her and across the aisle from her.

BUS DRIVER: Let me have those seats.

NARRATOR: At first no one stood up. Then the bus driver spoke again.

BUS DRIVER: You all better make it light on yourselves and give me those seats.

NARRATOR: The other three people stand up, but Rosa Parks remains seated.

BUS DRIVER: (*to Rosa Parks*) Are you going to stand?

ROSA PARKS: No, Sir, I'm not.

BUS DRIVER: If you don't stand up, I'll call the police and have you arrested.

ROSA PARKS: I understand.

NARRATOR: With that, the bus driver gets off the bus. Passengers begin whispering to each other.

FIRST PASSENGER: I wonder what's going to happen.

SECOND PASSENGER: I don't know.

FIRST PASSENGER: I'm not going to stay around to find out. I'm getting off this bus.

THIRD PASSENGER: Look, here comes the bus driver with two policemen.

FIRST POLICEMAN: (to Rosa Parks) Did the driver ask you to stand?

ROSA PARKS: Yes, he did.

FIRST POLICEMAN: Well, why didn't you stand?

ROSA PARKS: I don't think I should have to stand up. Why do you all push us around?

FIRST POLICEMAN: I don't know, but the law's the law, and you're under arrest.

NARRATOR: Rosa Parks stands up when the policeman tells her that she is under arrest. They get off the bus and the two policemen walk her to the police car. One carries her purse, the other her shopping bag.

SCENE 2

NARRATOR: At the police station, Rosa Parks calls Mr. E. D. Nixon, who is former president of the state and local NAACP.

ROSA PARKS: Hello, Mr. Nixon. This is Rosa Parks. I'm calling to let you know that I've been arrested for refusing to give up my bus seat.

MR. E. D. NIXON: You are one brave woman, Mrs. Parks. I'll be right there to post bail. Then we'll see what we can do.

NARRATOR: Mrs. Parks was released from jail. Mr. Nixon called Rev. Ralph Abernathy and Rev. Martin Luther King, Jr., and the three started planning the famous bus boycott in Montgomery, Alabama. It was the beginning of the civil rights movement. Eventually, the buses in Montgomery were successfully desegregated.

ARTHUR A. SCHOMBURG

Do you like to solve mysteries? Arthur A. Schomburg sure did.

From the time he was a boy in Puerto Rico until his death in New York years later, he conducted a lifelong search for "missing persons." He believed that proper credit had not been given to many of the accomplishments of black people throughout history. The names and deeds of black kings and queens, explorers, mathematicians, inventors, philosophers, and artists were relatively unknown. Yet these persons had made great contributions.

Schomburg felt it was important for everyone to know about the achievements of these "missing persons." Learning about these achievers would have special meaning to people of African ancestry. They would have these people as role models. They would know that other black people had accomplished great things, and they could do the same if they tried.

Armed with only a few clues, Schomburg's search was especially difficult because when he began, even he did not know the names of many of the people he was trying to find.

Arthur Alfonso Schomburg was born in San Juan, Puerto

Rico, on January 24, 1874. Little is known about his early years, but it is known that his parents were Charles Schomburg and Mary Joseph. His father was a merchant whose father probably came to Puerto Rico from Hamburg, Germany, and married Maria Monserrate Bercedonis of Aguadilla, Puerto Rico. His mother was a washerwoman and a midwife. Her parents were from St. Croix in the Virgin Islands.

Information about Schomburg's education is sketchy. The accounts of his life do not agree about the amount of education he received. Most say that he was largely self-taught. He spent a lot of time around the cigar workers of Puerto Rico. According to one source, the cigar workers helped teach him his ABCs.

At some point in his growing-up years, he went to the Virgin Islands to live with his mother's father, Nicholas Joseph. He probably attended the College of St. Thomas during this period.

He returned to San Juan on at least one occasion. While there he participated in an interracial history club. The members of the club were all social equals. Schomburg noted, however, that the white members knew and took pride in their history. The members of African ancestry were not as familiar with their history. Not knowing their history, they could not draw inspiration from it.

This prompted Schomburg to learn all he could so that he could speak knowledgeably. At first he read all he could about the history of black Puerto Ricans. He noted that "The works of José Julian Acosta and Salvador Brau have been my first inspiration to a further and intense study of the Negro." His study soon broadened and he began to try to unearth the

history of Africans and their descendants in the Caribbean and elsewhere around the world.

Like every good detective, he followed every clue. He would write down every fact he could find. The more he looked for information, the more he was able to find. Schomburg believed it was important to have evidence—to be able to show proof— of things black people had accomplished. He was not only interested in history. He was interested in every kind of black self-expression. He collected documents, manuscripts, poems, plays, sermons, letters, music, and artwork.

Schomburg traveled far and wide in his effort to find evidence of the worldwide African presence. He conducted a tireless search of the book markets of the United States, Latin America, and Europe. Once when in Spain, he used his knowledge of black Spanish artists and slavery to do some superb detective work that probably no one else in the world was in a position to do. He located a long-lost picture by artist Juan de Pareja.

It was in April of 1891 when Arthur Schomburg moved to New York City. He lived in the community of Puerto Rican and Cuban cigar workers and artisans. At that time, both Puerto Rico and Cuba were Spanish colonies. Schomburg's neighbors belonged to political organizations that worked to free their homelands from Spanish rule.

Soon after Schomburg landed in New York he went to see Flor Baerga, a leader in the Caribbean independence movement and an amateur book collector. Schomburg shared Baerga's political philosophy and his interest in collecting.

By 1926, Schomburg had 11,000 books and other items he had collected. He had financed his purchases with his earnings. His first job in New York was in the law offices of Pryor, Mellis, and Harris. After five years he went to work for Bankers Trust Company on Wall Street and he remained there for twenty-three years.

Throughout these years Schomburg spoke and wrote about his abiding interest in books. One of the things he did was to compile a bibliography. His essay, "The Negro Digs Up His Past," appeared in Alain Locke's book, *The New Negro*. In 1911, Locke and John E. Bruce had founded the Negro Society for Historical Research. They published a paper in which Schomburg made a plea for more African and African-American history to be taught in schools and colleges.

Meanwhile, Schomburg's private collection had become so extensive and so highly respected that the National Urban League worked out an arrangement with the Carnegie Corporation to purchase the collection for the New York Public Library system. Carnegie paid $10,000. The collection was to remain intact and be housed at the 135th Street library.

This agreement fulfilled two of Schomburg's wishes. He had wanted the collection to be accessible to students of black history, and to provide inspiration to black writers. His collection became a valuable resource for students and writers during the Harlem Renaissance—that period of new ideas by leading black writers and artists in the 1920s. This was typical of Schomburg, for he had always been very generous about sharing his books.

In 1927, Schomburg received the William E. Harmon Award for outstanding work in the field of education. In 1929, he retired from his job on Wall Street and became the curator of a collection at Fisk University in Nashville, Tennessee. He built up the Fisk collection to include every kind of information from Ashanti customs to Zulu nursery rhymes.

In 1932, another gift from the Carnegie Corporation made it possible for the New York Public Library to hire Schomburg to be reunited with his collection. He became the curator of the Division of Negro Literature, History, and Prints. He remained there—doing the work he loved most—until his death in June, 1938. After his death, the division was renamed the Schomburg Collection of Negro Literature and History. In 1973, it became the Schomburg Center for Research in Black Culture.

Today the Schomburg Center—which is located at 135th Street and Lenox Avenue in New York City—has the world's largest and most complete collection of material about the history, writings, and art of black people.

Arthur Alfonso Schomburg had started out looking for "missing persons" in black history. He found and collected proof that black people had made great achievements. Then he shared his findings.

On a more personal note, Schomburg was widowed twice. His first wife, the former Elizabeth Hatcher from Virginia, died in 1902. His second wife, Elizabeth Marrow Taylor from North Carolina, died in 1909. He was survived by his third wife, Elizabeth Green, one daughter, and seven sons.

Arthur A. Schomburg's legacy is stated in the essay he wrote in *The New Negro*: "History must restore what slavery took away, for it is the social damage of slavery that the present generation must repair and offset."

A Legacy of Dignity and Pride

🐌

CAST

First Narrator   Second Student
Second Narrator   Librarian
First Student

FIRST NARRATOR: It is a bright Saturday morning in New York City. Two students who are classmates and best friends are crossing the street at 135th Street and Lenox Avenue. The Schomburg Center for Research in Black Culture is on that corner. The children pause to read the sign on the front of the building, then walk on. They are on their way to the Countee Cullen public library which is around the corner on 136th Street.

SECOND NARRATOR: The children have passed the Schomburg Center many times before, but they're especially curious about it today because they have a school assignment to find out who Arthur A. Schomburg was. They talk as they walk along.

FIRST STUDENT: Do you suppose that big, pretty building is named for the man the teacher told us to find out about?

SECOND STUDENT: Maybe. Schomburg is an unusual name. I never heard of it anywhere except on that building.

FIRST STUDENT: I never thought about it much before.

SECOND STUDENT: Me neither.

FIRST STUDENT: I've heard that some kind of library is in that building.

SECOND STUDENT: Me, too. But have you noticed? You never see kids going in there—only adults.

FIRST STUDENT: (*thinking a minute*) You're right.

FIRST NARRATOR: The children arrive at their destination.

SECOND NARRATOR: The Countee Cullen branch of the New York Public Library.

SECOND STUDENT: You noticed the teacher said to come to the Countee Cullen library to find out about Schomburg. She didn't say, "Go to the Schomburg Center."

FIRST STUDENT: I wonder why.

FIRST NARRATOR: The children walk to the children's department in the library.

SECOND NARRATOR: They walk over to the librarian's desk.

LIBRARIAN: May I help you?

SECOND STUDENT: Yesterday our teacher gave us a school assignment.

FIRST STUDENT: She told us to get information about a man named Arthur A. Schomburg.

SECOND STUDENT: Is that the Schomburg that the Schomburg Center is named for?

LIBRARIAN: Yes, it surely is.

FIRST STUDENT: Wow, he must have been famous!

SECOND STUDENT: How did he get a big building like that named for him?

LIBRARIAN: Actually he is not as well known as he deserves to be. Still, he left quite a legacy. Eventually more people will learn about his work.

FIRST STUDENT: What did he do?

LIBRARIAN: Well, he personally collected enough books to start a library.

SECOND STUDENT: How do you mean?

LIBRARIAN: He spent his entire life reading and collecting books. He was particularly interested in the history and contributions of black people anywhere in the world. But books on this subject were so hard to find that he had to search everywhere.

FIRST STUDENT: Everywhere?

LIBRARIAN: Everywhere he could find information.

SECOND STUDENT: Did he even go out of the United States looking for information about black people?

LIBRARIAN: Yes, he traveled and searched far and wide. He found books and information that even college professors hadn't heard about.

FIRST STUDENT: Wow, he must have had thousands of books.

LIBRARIAN: He really did. In 1926, he owned 11,000 books and pieces of art.

SECOND STUDENT: I see why you said he had enough books to start a library.

FIRST STUDENT: Where are all his books now?

LIBRARIAN: They're in the Schomburg Center right around the corner. About 75,000 more books have been added to the original collection. Some were collected by Schomburg and others were donated or purchased.

SECOND STUDENT: Those books must have been worth a lot of money.

LIBRARIAN: They were. In fact, back in 1926 the Carnegie Corporation bought Schomburg's original collection for $10,000— which must have seemed like a million dollars in those days.

FIRST STUDENT: What happened to the books then?

LIBRARIAN: They were given to the New York Public Library.

SECOND STUDENT: Didn't Schomburg get lonesome for his books? I would think if I'd spent a long time collecting something, I'd miss it when it was gone—even if I got a lot of money for it.

LIBRARIAN: I guess Schomburg felt the same way you would. Fortunately, he eventually got to be the curator—the person to take care of—his collection.

FIRST NARRATOR: Thinking about the fact that all those books are in a building right next door, the First Student asks the Librarian a question.

FIRST STUDENT: Could we go over to the Schomburg Center and see all those books?

SECOND STUDENT: We never see kids going in there. Can't they go there?

LIBRARIAN: Yes, children can go into that library—if they go with an adult.

FIRST STUDENT: Why is that? We can come in this library by ourselves.

LIBRARIAN: Well, the Schomburg is a different kind of library. It's what you call a research center. Most people who go there have read all the things they can find at a regular library like this. The Schomburg has some rare books you can't find any place else. So writers and history teachers and other people who want to learn all they possibly can about African-American history and culture go there to study. People come from far and wide to study there.

FIRST STUDENT: What would happen if somebody came from far away and when they got there they found that the book they wanted had been checked out?

LIBRARIAN: Well, that's another difference between the Schomburg and a regular library. The books there can't be checked out. That way they are always there whenever someone needs them.

SECOND STUDENT: (*disappointedly*) So that means that even if we got a grown-up to take us there, all we could do is just look at books on a shelf, right?

LIBRARIAN: No, the Schomburg has more than just books. It has films, artwork, and music. It even has manuscripts of famous writers like Countee Cullen, the man this library was named for.

FIRST STUDENT: Really?

SECOND STUDENT: We already know about Countee Cullen. He was a famous poet.

LIBRARIAN: Right. The Schomburg Center has some of the works of Countee Cullen, Langston Hughes, and many other great black writers.

FIRST STUDENT: That's interesting.

SECOND STUDENT: It sure is.

LIBRARIAN: What I think you'll find even more interesting are the Schomburg exhibitions. (*picking up a little booklet on her desk*) Here's a brochure that tells all about the next exhibition.

FIRST STUDENT: (*opening the booklet*) What kind of exhibition is it?

LIBRARIAN: Well, it's a big exhibit—with pictures, and books, and all kinds of materials on display. The first night there is always a wonderful reception when lots of people, including some famous ones, come and visit and look at the exhibit.

SECOND STUDENT: Have you ever gone to one of those receptions?

LIBRARIAN: Oh, yes. Many times. And every time it is a really special evening.

FIRST STUDENT: I'd like that. You said that kids could go with an adult. I'm going to ask my mom to take us when the next exhibit opens.

SECOND STUDENT: (*remembering their school assignment*) We could find out something about Arthur Schomburg that way.

LIBRARIAN: You could make a start right here. There are not too many books with information about Schomburg. I hope there are more someday. But let me get you an encyclopedia. That will tell you something about him. And you will still have the exhibition to look forward to.

FIRST STUDENT: I'm sure glad the teacher told us to look up Mr. Schomburg.

SECOND STUDENT: Me, too!

LEONTYNE PRICE

IT WAS THE LOVE OF MUSIC that transformed Mary Violet Leontyne Price from a schoolgirl in a tiny Mississippi town to Leontyne Price, star of opera houses around the world.

Leontyne was born on February 10, 1927, in Laurel, Mississippi. She grew up loving music. Her parents were musical. They sang in the choir and played in the band at St. Paul's Methodist Church. They recognized their daughter's interest in music. They saw to it that she had an opportunity to listen to recordings. They arranged for Leontyne and her brother George to take piano lessons from Miss Hattie V. J. McKenna. A favorite aunt, called Big Auntie, was sure that Leontyne was a child prodigy.

Leontyne played the piano and the organ at church. She also sang there and at community events. At the age of nine and a half, her mother took her to the city of Jackson to hear Marian Anderson, the well-known black contralto, sing in concert. Seeing and hearing Miss Anderson made a deep and lasting impression on Leontyne. "It was one of the most enthralling, marvelous experiences I've ever had," she said later.

"I can't tell you how inspired I was to do something similar to what she was doing."

Leontyne kept this dream, even though the likelihood of realizing it come true was very slim. In 1944, Leontyne graduated from Oak Park High School. Her parents mortgaged their home so that she could go to Central State College in Ohio. Being practical, she took courses that would prepare her to become a music teacher. But she also began her vocal studies. A high point of her college years was a meeting with the great black baritone singer, Paul Robeson. Leontyne was a soloist on his program.

Following college, Leontyne was awarded a four-year scholarship to the Juilliard School of Music in New York City. A former concert singer, Florence Page Kimball, became her vocal coach there. She remained a close consultant for years.

Living in New York City was costly, and her scholarship was for tuition only. Leontyne found that her part-time desk clerk job was not enough to cover living expenses. Working while going to school was not a new experience for her. During college, she had worked in the cafeteria during the school year. During school vacations, she had worked as a maid and sometimes sung for parties in the home of a wealthy white family in her hometown of Laurel. It was that wealthy family, the Chisholms, who provided some financial assistance, as they often did for young people in Laurel, both black and white. This made it possible for Leontyne to spend her time studying, rather than earning money singing in nightclubs as some students did.

Leontyne's singing ability was quickly recognized. While

still at Juilliard, composer Virgil Thompson heard her and was so impressed that he asked her to appear in his opera, *Four Saints in Three Acts*. She made her debut on Broadway in that production in 1952, and went to Paris as a member of the cast. This led to Ira Gershwin's choosing her to sing Bess in the revival of *Porgy and Bess*. It played in New York City for two years, then made a highly successful international tour sponsored by the U.S. State Department. William Warfield was the male lead in this production. He and Leontyne married, but their respective careers kept them both so busy they later decided to divorce.

In 1955, Leontyne Price sang a triumphant performance in the title role of *Tosca* for the television production of this opera. Millions of viewers saw and heard her in this and in other TV opera appearances. Her "live" opera debut was with the San Francisco Opera in 1957 in Poulenc's *Dialogues of the Carmelites*. In succeeding seasons she appeared at the Chicago Lyric Opera and in other performances in San Francisco.

By 1960, Leontyne Price was considered one of the most popular lyric sopranos in the country. She had appeared in Vienna, and also at Milan's famous La Scala opera house where she performed the leading role in Verdi's *Aida*. An Italian critic gave her the highest praise by saying, "Our great Verdi would have found her the ideal Aida."

It was 1961 when Leontyne Price's childhood dream came true. She made her debut at the great Metropolitan Opera in New York City, singing the role of Leonora in Verdi's *Il Trovatore*. Singing major roles at the Metropolitan Opera House is one of the highest accomplishments a singer can achieve.

The music critics and opera-goers loved her. The "Met" became her home. Leontyne Price was a star. She appeared there 119 times between 1961 and 1969. When the new Metropolitan Opera House was opened at Lincoln Center, she was chosen to star in the premiere of Samuel Barber's opera, *Antony and Cleopatra*. Worldwide attention was focused on her.

In 1985, when Leontyne Price retired from the Met, she continued to give recitals and make recordings. Music lovers can hear her in complete operas, Christmas songs, Negro spirituals, and art songs.

Leontyne Price has received many honorary awards from universities. She was also awarded the Presidential Freedom Medal (1964), the Italian Award of Merit (1965), and the Spingarn Medal given by the National Association for the Advancement of Colored People (NAACP). But she has not been content to excell and receive honors. She has remembered her "roots." She has contributed her time and resources to younger singers, to civil rights groups, and to her family church in her beloved hometown of Laurel, Mississippi.

The Priceless Leontyne

20

CAST

Big Auntie   Usher
Guest   First Narrator
Friend of Guest   Second Narrator

Note: If anyone else wants to be in the skit, they can play the roles of choir members (facing the congregation) or church members sitting in the audience.

FIRST NARRATOR: An out-of-town Guest has happened to sit down beside Big Auntie in church. The friend she has come to visit is singing in the choir. The congregation is singing and Leontyne Price is accompanying them on the organ.

SECOND NARRATOR: The Guest has been watching Leontyne with great interest. She is so intrigued that she finally whispers to Big Auntie.

GUEST: Excuse me, but do you happen to know that young lady who is playing the organ?

BIG AUNTIE: (*with a smile*) Yes, she's my niece!

GUEST: My, she certainly seems talented.

BIG AUNTIE: We're real proud of her.

FIRST NARRATOR: An usher comes to the end of the pew where Big Auntie and the Guest are seated.

SECOND NARRATOR: The usher passes the collection plate to the Guest. She puts money in the plate and passes it to Big Auntie, then back to the usher.

FIRST NARRATOR: Meantime, Leontyne has moved over to the piano and is playing for the youth choir. The Guest is impressed.

GUEST: (*whispering to Big Auntie*) My, now she is playing the piano. I'd like to hear more about her after the service.

BIG AUNTIE: All right.

FIRST NARRATOR: The minister begins his sermon and Big Auntie and the Guest listen as he speaks.

SECOND NARRATOR: The senior choir begins to sing a selection after the sermon. Big Auntie nudges the Guest and points to the soloist.

BIG AUNTIE: See the woman singing the solo? That's Leontyne's mother.

GUEST: Really?

FIRST NARRATOR: Soon church was over. Big Auntie and the Guest walk up the aisle together.

GUEST: My, I just can't get over how talented your niece is. You must be very proud of her.

BIG AUNTIE: I certainly am. I feel like she's something of a musical genius. She sings, too.

GUEST: Has she always shown a talent for music?

BIG AUNTIE: Yes, ever since she was real small.

GUEST: Has she had formal training or did she just pick it up?

BIG AUNTIE: Well, she picked it up at first, but since then she and her brother have taken piano lessons from Miss Hattie McKenna.

GUEST: Has she shown any interest in making a career of music?

BIG AUNTIE: Yes, she's been talking about studying to be a music teacher when she grows up.

GUEST: It looks to me as if she has the talent to perform, rather than limiting herself to teaching. Has she ever had a chance to go to a recital where she could hear classical music?

BIG AUNTIE: Yes, when she was nine, her mother took her over to Jackson to hear Marian Anderson sing.

GUEST: How did she like it?

BIG AUNTIE: She loved it. She came home raving about how dignified Marian Anderson was, and how beautiful her voice was.

GUEST: That's great. I won't be surprised if that young lady grows up to be as well known for her music as Marian Anderson is.

BIG AUNTIE: That would be wonderful.

SECOND NARRATOR: The Guest spots the woman she's visiting coming down from the choir loft.

GUEST: Oh, there's my friend. You must surely know her. (*to the friend who has joined them*) Oh, I've just been hearing all about this lady's niece. She certainly is musical!

FRIEND OF GUEST: That would be Leontyne. You should hear her sing!

GUEST: I bet she is just as good at that as she is at playing the organ and the piano.

FRIEND OF GUEST: She certainly is. She has real talent.

FIRST NARRATOR: The church service is over, and Big Auntie and the Guest and her friend say good-bye.

GUEST: Well, it's certainly been nice talking with you.

BIG AUNTIE: (*to Guest*) Thank you. It's been nice talking with you, too.

GUEST: I do hope that niece of yours gets a chance to develop her musical talents.

BIG AUNTIE: I hope so. I'm sure going to do everything I can to encourage her.

FIRST NARRATOR: And, as you know, Leontyne Price certainly did develop her talent in music—especially singing.

SECOND NARRATOR: She went on to become a world-famous opera singer.

CHARLES WHITE

ARTIST CHARLES WHITE got his first set of oil paints when he was seven years old. His first canvases were his mother's window shades. His easel was the back of a chair in a crowded apartment in Chicago. Even at that early age, he was serious about painting. He knew that when he grew up he wanted to be a fine painter.

Charles White was born in Chicago on April 2, 1918, as World War I was coming to an end. His parents, like so many other southern blacks, had come north seeking jobs, education for their children, a better life. But life in the North was not all they hoped it would be. There were housing problems, labor disputes, race riots.

Charles White's father was a Creek Indian from Georgia who was a railroad worker and steelworker. He died when Charles was eight years old. His mother, Ethel Gary White, was African-American. Her family came from Trinidad and had been taken as slaves to Mississippi. In Chicago she worked as a maid and often took Charles to work with her so that he would not be left at home alone. She bought paints for him so he could entertain himself while she was working, but Charles enjoyed painting so much that he painted on things he wasn't supposed to. Before long his mother took his paints away. She gave him a violin instead.

One day when Charles was walking home from Burke Elementary School, he passed an outdoor art class. He stopped to watch, and the students showed him how to mix paints. He came away with a renewed interest in painting. Even in grade school he had part-time jobs—shoeshine boy, messenger—to help out the family income. But he never put aside his interest in painting. Sometimes he stopped at the library to admire the paintings there. He especially liked those of Winslow Homer.

Charles won a nationwide pencil sketching contest while in high school. After a number of disappointments caused by racial prejudice, he won a one-year scholarship at the Art Institute of Chicago. There were art lectures and demonstrations and homework assignments. His work often received high marks.

Charles loved to read and he discovered one book in particular that helped shape his future—*The New Negro* by Alain Locke. It gave him a new appreciation of the richness of black literature and history. He wished his high school taught courses about things like that.

Although that wish didn't come true, his high school art teachers encouraged him to enter competitions. He won some scholarships and was able to continue his studies, though he had to work at other jobs to manage. But once equipped with an art school education and the talents he already had, Charles felt ready to become a full-fledged artist. The problem was that the country was still feeling the effects of the Great Depression. There were very few jobs available.

Luckily, the Works Progress Administration provided work for artists. White and many other young artists welcomed the opportunity to beautify public buildings. One of White's first paintings was done for the Chicago Public Library. He taught courses and had his work exhibited, and then won a grant from the Julius Rosenwald Foundation.

In 1941, Charles White married accomplished black sculptor Alice Elizabeth Catlett. The Rosenwald grant made it possible for them to spend two years traveling and working in the South. They got a firsthand view of what life was like for southern black people. White's work is best known for drawings which show the contributions and dignity of black people. His work was called "social art" because it depicted the struggles and endurance of these people. A mural he did at Hampton Institute is called *The Contribution of the Negro to American Democracy*.

His career seemed off to a good start when World War II began and White was drafted into the army. He contracted tuberculosis and spent three years in the hospital. When discharged, he returned to his painting.

A one-man show in New York received much praise. Then Charles White and his wife went to Mexico to work and study with leading artists there. He was impressed with their use of black and white. He was able to paint powerful pictures without using many colors. He made skillful use of black and white to dramatize highlights, shadows, soft lines, draped fabric, or wrinkles.

Returning to the United States, White became artist-in-residence at Howard University. A failing marriage and health problems altered his plans. After a divorce and five lung operations, he went to New York.

Charles White always tried to honor black people and their efforts in his paintings. Some of his most famous works are *Let's Walk Together*, the *Gospel Singer*, and black heroes. White died in October, 1979, spending his last years in Altadena, California, but he got to see his work recognized. Prizes and awards and medals came his way. His work can be found in many countries around the world, and it is on display in many collections in the United States. He was on the executive board of the Black Academy of Arts and Letters. He taught and chaired the department of drawing at the Otis Institute of Art until shortly before his death.

Mrs. Ethel Gary White could never have envisioned what an important gift she gave her son, Charles, on his seventh birthday.

A Turning Point in the Life of Charles White

৵

CAST

Charles White First Student
First Narrator Second Student
Second Narrator Third Student
Instructor

FIRST NARRATOR: *Setting*: the South Side of Chicago

SECOND NARRATOR: One day—a Monday perhaps—as Charles White started home from Burke Elementary School, he noticed some people painting pictures across the street in Washington Park.

FIRST NARRATOR: Charles loved painting more than anything else in the world. He'd loved it since his seventh birthday when his mother had given him a set of paints, but . . .

SECOND NARRATOR: Charles had been so eager to paint that he painted on the window shades. His mother didn't like that a bit, so she took the paints away from him and encouraged him to play the violin instead.

FIRST NARRATOR: After that, school was the only place Charles got a chance to paint. Although Miss Mary Ryan was an excellent art teacher, that wasn't enough to satisfy him. So when he saw people painting in the park he went right over there.

SECOND NARRATOR: Charles is spellbound as he observes the painters, their equipment, and their paintings.

FIRST STUDENT: (*seeing Charles's interested and longing look*) Hello, there.

CHARLES: Hello.

FIRST STUDENT: What's your name?

CHARLES: Charles . . .

FIRST STUDENT: I see you're interested in our paintings. Do you know how to paint?

CHARLES: (*shyly*) Yes, a little . . .

FIRST STUDENT: Well, would you like to learn more about it?

CHARLES: (*enthusiastically*) Oh, yes!

FIRST STUDENT: Well, we're all students at an art school for grown-ups, but we're going to be working in the park all week. I bet our instructor wouldn't mind if you came over after school each day.

CHARLES: Really?

FIRST STUDENT: Yes. Would you like that?

CHARLES: Oh, yes!

FIRST STUDENT: Wait here a minute. Let me check to make sure it's all right with my instructor.

FIRST NARRATOR: The student goes and talks with the instructor, then comes back to talk with Charles.

FIRST STUDENT: The instructor says it's fine. See you tomorrow.

CHARLES: (*happily*) Thanks! See you tomorrow!

SECOND NARRATOR: It's Tuesday. All day Charles has been anxious for school to get out so he can head for the park.

FIRST STUDENT: Hello, Charles. I see you came back. You're welcome to sit here and watch me work or you can walk around and see what the other students are doing.

CHARLES: Thank you. I think I'd like to watch you work today. Maybe I'll walk around tomorrow.

FIRST STUDENT: (*understanding that Charles is shy, changes the subject to painting*) This type of picture is called a landscape . . .

FIRST NARRATOR: It's Wednesday. Charles watched intently as the art student worked. He carefully studied what the first student did the first day. By the next day he felt comfortable going to watch the other students.

SECOND NARRATOR: All the students were friendly, chatting with Charles as they worked.

SECOND STUDENT TO THIRD STUDENT: (*noticing how serious Charles is*) Have you ever seen another child take that kind of interest in painting?

THIRD STUDENT: No, I was thinking the same thing.

SECOND STUDENT: As interested as he is, I bet he could catch on quickly if we gave him a few tips.

THIRD STUDENT: I bet so too. Charles, have you learned about primary colors in school?

CHARLES: Yes—they're red, yellow, and blue.

THIRD STUDENT: Right!

SECOND STUDENT: Do you know the secondary colors?

CHARLES: Yes—orange, purple, and green.

SECOND STUDENT: Have you ever mixed oil paint to make those colors?

CHARLES: No, I haven't. I've never used oil paint. But I've mixed watercolors and tempera paint.

THIRD STUDENT: Well, it's the same idea. What two colors would you mix together to get green?

CHARLES: Yellow and blue.

SECOND STUDENT: Well, here, I'll squirt a little of each on my palette and you can mix them.

CHARLES: *(intrigued by this, mixes the paint and when he's finished says)* There, how's that?

SECOND STUDENT: Just fine. Do you know how to make more of a blue-green?

CHARLES: Just add more blue?

SECOND STUDENT: Right.

CHARLES: Suppose I wanted a real pale green?

THIRD STUDENT: Just add white paint until you get the shade you want. Here (*squirting some white paint beside the green Charles has just mixed*). See how many shades of green you can make.

CHARLES: (*working until he has about fifteen shades of green*) This is fun!

FIRST NARRATOR: It's Thursday. Charles has gone back every single day.

INSTRUCTOR: Hello, Charles. The students were telling me what a good job you did mixing paint yesterday. You have the makings of an artist. I wouldn't be surprised if you grew up to be famous someday.

CHARLES: Thank you. I'd like that.

SECOND NARRATOR: It's Friday, the last day of the class.

FIRST STUDENT: Hello, Charles. Have you enjoyed the class this week?

CHARLES: Yes, thank you for letting me come. I really liked it.

FIRST STUDENT: Well, I'm glad. Do you have any questions about anything you've seen us do?

CHARLES: Yes, what is that smelly stuff you use to thin the paint or clean your brushes?

FIRST STUDENT: That's turpentine. It's also handy if you make a mistake on a painting. You can use it kind of like you'd use an eraser on paper.

CHARLES: I didn't know that. I've learned a lot this week. I'm sorry this is your last day.

FIRST STUDENT: I'm sorry, too, but we have finished landscape painting. Monday we'll go back to having classes in the art school. And, like you said, you've learned a lot this week. Keep practicing on your own and whenever you have the chance to take classes, do that.

CHARLES: I will. Thank you again.

FIRST STUDENT: You're welcome.

CHARLES: Good-bye.

FIRST STUDENT: Good-bye, Charles—and good luck with your art.

GARRETT A. MORGAN

EVERYONE WHO HAS EVER crossed a street safely with the help of a traffic light can thank Garrett A. Morgan. He is the inventor who thought of a way for people and cars to take turns crossing at intersections.

Garrett A. Morgan was born in Paris, Tennessee, on March 4, 1875. His parents, Sydney and Elizabeth Reed Morgan, had ten other children. Times were hard and at age fourteen Morgan struck out on his own—heading for nearby Cincinnati, Ohio. He found a job as a handyman.

Four years later he moved to Cleveland, Ohio. He arrived with only a quarter to his name, but he had a talent for fixing mechanical things—and for saving his money. He got a job as a sewing machine adjuster at the Roots and McBride Company. Before long he had thought of an idea. It was a belt fastener for sewing machines.

Garrett Morgan soon saved enough money to buy his own sewing machine business and purchase a home. His father had died by that time and he invited his mother to move to Cleveland. A year later he married Mary Anne Hassek. They

enjoyed a long, happy marriage and were the parents of three sons.

Morgan was a good businessman. Before long he was able to open a tailoring shop in which he hired thirty-two employees. His shop made suits, dresses, and coats with sewing equipment he had built.

Although planning was important to his success, his next business venture came about by accident. He was trying to find a liquid chemical that he could use to polish sewing machines. While he was experimenting, his wife called him to dinner. Hurriedly, he wiped his hands on a pony-fur cloth on his workbench and the wiry fur hairs straightened out. Curious to see how this liquid would affect other kinds of hair, he tried it out on the Airedale dog next door. The dog's hair got so straight that his owner hardly recognized him. After a bit more experimenting, Morgan put the chemical on the market as a product to straighten hair.

His next invention was a safety hood or "breathing device." In more recent years it has been called a gas mask. Morgan received a patent for it (U.S. Patent No. 1,113,675) and as he stated: "The object of the invention is to provide a portable attachment which will enable a fireman to enter a house filled with thick suffocating gases and smoke and to breathe freely for sometime therein, and thereby enable him to perform his duties of saving life and valuables without danger to himself from suffocation."

The safety hood won a first prize gold medal from the International Exposition for Sanitation and Safety. The judges at the exposition immediately recognized its value. Morgan wanted to market his invention, but he believed prejudice would limit his sales if his racial identity was generally known. He knew that some fire departments would rather endanger their firemen's lives than do business with a black inventor. He attempted to solve this problem in a most unusual way. He formed the National Safety Device Company. He was the only nonwhite officer. The other officers—one of whom had been the director of public works for the city of Cleveland— would arrange for demonstrations of the device and set up a canvas tent in the demonstration area. They would set a fire in the tent with an awful-smelling fuel made of tar, sulphur, formaldehyde, and manure. Once the fire was roaring, Morgan would appear disguised as an Indian chief. He'd put on the gas mask and go in and remain up to twenty minutes while he extinguished the flames. He would come out as good as new. This might have gone on indefinitely, but the night of July 25, 1916, changed everything. Morgan became a hero overnight.

That night there was a violent explosion at the Cleveland Waterworks. Approximately thirty workmen were trapped in a tunnel five miles out and more than 225 feet beneath Lake Erie. Smoke, natural gases, and debris kept would-be rescuers from entering the tunnel where the workmen were trapped. Family and friends didn't know whether anyone had survived the blast.

Finally, someone at the site of this disaster remembered that Garrett Morgan had invented a gas mask. It was about two o'clock in the morning when Morgan was called in. He, his brother Frank, and two volunteers put on gas masks and entered the tunnel. They were able to save the surviving work-men, including the superintendent, whom Morgan revived with artificial respiration.

Newspaper wire services picked up the story. The account of Morgan's heroism appeared in papers across the country. This turned out to be a mixed blessing. The city of Cleveland awarded Morgan a diamond-studded gold medal for heroism. Safety hoods or gas masks were ordered by the U.S. government. Many American, English, and German veterans of World War I owe their lives to the gas masks. Chemists, engineers, and other people working with noxious fumes could work more safely. At first, many fire departments ordered gas

masks for use in their work, but because of racial prejudice, the number of orders dwindled, and some orders were cancelled when it became known that Morgan was a black man. Meanwhile, Thomas A. Farrell, Cleveland's Director of Public Utilities, wrote to the Carnegie Hero Fund Commission to inform them of Morgan's heroic deed. The Commission had been endowed by Andrew Carnegie to reward people who had shown great heroism. Instead of awarding Garrett Morgan, the Commission gave the hero medal to the project superintendent whose life Morgan had saved. People who knew that Morgan deserved this honor realized this was very unfair.

Instead of being discouraged, Garrett Morgan went back to his drawing board. Without the disappointment of the gas mask, he might never have developed his next invention, the stoplight. While the gas mask saved the lives of people who did dangerous work, the traffic light has saved the lives of drivers and pedestrians—of all ages, all across the world.

Reportedly, Morgan was the first black person in Cleveland to own a car. As the number of cars increased, there was a need for an effective way to control the flow of traffic. Intersections were especially dangerous. Morgan put his problem-solving skills to work and invented the three-way automatic electric stoplight. It didn't look like today's stoplight, but it provided the concept on which modern stoplights are based. For some time, railroads had used a semaphore or signaling system. Train engineers could look straight down the track and tell from the position of the semaphore whether to stop or proceed. Since city streets intersect, Morgan had to come up with a way to signal drivers on side streets as well as main thoroughfares. He received his patent (U.S. Patent No. 1,475,024) on November 20, 1923. At first, Morgan marketed the invention himself, but then decided to sell rights to the General Electric Company for $40,000. He not only had quite a lot more money than he had when he arrived in Cleveland— he had made two gigantic contributions to public safety.

Even though Garrett Morgan's contributions made life easier for everyone, regardless of race, he had been the victim of racism. Believing that no one should be denied opportunities because of their race, he worked to try to keep other people from having the kind of bad experiences he had had. He went about solving this problem in several different ways. He was concerned that the local newspapers didn't contain much news about the black community and things that were being accomplished there, so he started the *Cleveland Call* newspaper. (It is now known as the *Call and Post* and has a large circulation.) He was active in civil rights organizations. And feeling that black citizens were not properly represented in local government, he ran for City Council. Although he did not win that election, Cleveland later became the first large American city to elect a black man as mayor.

For the last twenty years of his life, Morgan suffered from glaucoma. This resulted in near-blindness, but it didn't slow down his sharp mind. Although he had hoped to attend the Emancipation Centennial to be held in Chicago in August, 1963, Garrett Morgan died less than a month before that event. But he had lived to receive a well-deserved honor. Six months before his death he was cited by the United States government for having invented the first traffic signal.

Meet the Inventor of the Stoplight

&

CAST

First Narrator	Reporter
Second Narrator	Student
Garrett Morgan	

FIRST NARRATOR: It is rush hour on a Friday evening in a large city.

SECOND NARRATOR: A radio reporter and Mr. Garrett A. Morgan, inventor of the stoplight, are standing at a busy corner. They watch as cars stop on the red light, then drive away when the light turns green.

FIRST NARRATOR: It is time for a radio program to begin.

SECOND NARRATOR: The reporter adjusts his earphones and speaks into his microphone.

REPORTER: Hello, this is _____(*child playing this part gives his or her own name*), your roving reporter. My guest today is Mr. Garrett A. Morgan, the inventor of the stoplight.

REPORTER: (*speaking to the guest*) Mr. Morgan, how does it feel to know that your invention makes it possible for rush hour traffic to move smoothly and safely?

GARRETT MORGAN: I'm very pleased.

REPORTER: How did you happen to think of the idea?

GARRETT MORGAN: Well, I knew that trains used light signals, and I saw that every year there were more and more cars on the streets. There were sure to be more and more accidents, so I set out to design a signal that could . . .

REPORTER: . . . make drivers take turns?

GARRETT MORGAN: (*laughingly*) Yes! Sometimes drivers are in such a big hurry to get where they're going, they don't remember whether it is their turn or not.

REPORTER: I've heard that you invented the stoplight after an unhappy experience. Is that true?

GARRETT MORGAN: (*pausing as if he really doesn't want to talk about this*) Yes, it is. I had invented the safety hood or gas mask.

REPORTER: Is it true that you had not only invented the gas mask, but you personally rescued many of the workmen at the Cleveland Waterworks explosion?

GARRETT MORGAN: Yes, that's true.

REPORTER: You're modest, Mr. Morgan. Please tell our listeners what happened.

GARRETT MORGAN: Well, the blast trapped workmen more than 200 feet below Lake Erie. Tunnel Number Five was filled with smoke and gas.

REPORTER: Luckily, you lived in the same city and someone at the Waterworks had heard of your invention.

GARRETT MORGAN: Yes, I was called in about two o'clock in the morning. My brother and I put on gas masks and went down with two volunteers. And we brought up all the workmen who were still alive.

STUDENT: (*who has walked up in time to hear about this rescue*) Wow! You all were heroes!

GARRETT MORGAN: We were just glad to do what we could.

REPORTER: I would have thought that every fire department in the world would have bought gas masks after they heard you'd gone through all that smoke and gas unharmed.

GARRETT MORGAN: They did at first, but when they found out that the gas mask was invented by a black person, they stopped buying the masks.

REPORTER: Even though it might have saved their lives?

STUDENT: Oh, Mr. Morgan, really?

GARRETT MORGAN: Yes, but I didn't let it get me down. By that time I started working on the stoplight.

REPORTER: And your stoplight has made such a great contribution. Cities couldn't have handled all the traffic they have today without the stoplight.

STUDENT: Well, at least you do get recognized for inventing the stoplight. I'm really glad I stopped here today and got to meet you.

GARRETT MORGAN: Thank you.

REPORTER: Thank you, Mr. Morgan, for being with us today. Thank you even more for using your inventive genius to save so many lives.

DANIEL "CHAPPIE" JAMES

WHEN DANIEL "CHAPPIE" JAMES was a little boy he used to see airplanes take off from the Naval Air Base in his hometown of Pensacola, Florida. This was in the 1920s, and airplanes weren't as commonplace as they are now. The public was fascinated by flight. Like many other children, Daniel James watched, and wished that he could fly a plane when he grew up. There were, however, many hurdles he would have to overcome in order to become a pilot.

He not only overcame the hurdles that it took to become a pilot, he went on to become a four-star general. He was the first black American to hold this rank. Most people who knew the times and circumstances in which Daniel James was born would not have predicted that he'd reach those heights.

James never doubted himself, though, and that was the secret to his success. He developed a knack for being in the right place at the right time, and creating an influential role for himself wherever he went. If he was in a situation where people were in disagreement, he was often able to say something to help solve—or smooth over—the problem.

He got his confidence and other important character traits

from his parents. His father, Daniel James, Sr., was an ambitious, hardworking man who had come from Alabama to Florida as a migrant laborer. Once in Pensacola, he was able to improve his work situation. He found work as a lamplighter for the city of Pensacola. Later he took a job at the municipal gas plant. There he did skilled work and supervised other workers. He took his job and himself very seriously.

He set an example for his children as a person who didn't settle for second-best. He wasn't highly educated, but he wanted what he believed to be the best for his family. For example, he settled in a residential neighborhood rather than the Railroad Avenue area where migrant workers lived. He bought some other property, in addition to his home, and was a good provider for his family.

"Chappie" James's mother had grown up in Pensacola. She was a member of a family that had enjoyed opportunities and privileges that were not available to most black families. She had received a good education at St. Joseph's Catholic School. She firmly believed that the more education a black person had, the more opportunities he or she had. So she was determined that her children would have an excellent education. She was able to guarantee this, since she conducted her own private school in the family's backyard—even though she already had her hands full as the mother of seventeen children. Her standards were high, and being both mother and teacher, she was able to insist that her children strive for perfection. Her motto was what she called "the Eleventh Commandment": "Thou shalt never quit."

Daniel James took this advice to heart. Whenever he was

faced with a problem, he figured out a way to get through it rather than quit. One of the first problems he had to solve was what to do about his name. Being the youngest in the family, he was called "Dan Baby." He liked the special place he held in the family, but when he'd finished his mother's grade school and was about to enter high school, he wanted more of a he-man nickname. He borrowed his new nickname from an older brother, Charles, who had been an outstanding college athlete. "Chappie" was Charles's nickname, so "Dan Baby" started calling himself "Little Chappie," which was later shortened to "Chappie," especially when he became a strapping six feet, four inches.

Another problem James had to deal with was what to do when he was in situations where he did not excel. His self-confidence and desire to be popular enabled him to stick with a difficult situation and make the best of it. He wanted to play high school football. He liked the glory and attention the players enjoyed. Even though he was not the greatest player, his enthusiasm and his ability to encourage his teammates made him a well-liked member of the team. These personality traits helped him become "Big Man on Campus" when he entered college at Tuskegee Institute in Alabama. Most of the girls on campus admired him, but he married the one girl who was unimpressed with him. That was what made him pay attention to Dorothy Watkins. She was a shy girl who had grown up in the town of Tuskegee. It took "Chappie" four years to convince her he was as wonderful as everyone else thought he was.

Not only did James meet his bride at Tuskegee, it was there that "Chappie" first realized his childhood dream of learning to fly. In 1938—shortly before World War II—the Civilian Aeronautics Administration responded to the urging of black newspapers and the NAACP that blacks have the same opportunity as other Americans to qualify for the U.S. Air Corps. Flight training programs were set up at a number of black colleges to train civilian pilots. In March of 1941, Tuskegee Institute was chosen as the exclusive site for training black military pilots. "Chappie" James was in the right place at the right time. He excelled in the Civilian Pilot Training Program and the military's advanced flying program. Although there was a handful of individual black men and women who held private pilot's licenses, flight training had been generally inaccessible to black people. The "Tuskegee Experiment" provided the first real opportunity for black men to learn to fly. The cadets relished the challenge, and the success of the Tuskegee program was a great source of pride to black Americans.

As the Tuskegee pilots completed their training, they became commissioned officers in the United States Air Force. Many went into combat during World War II, serving in Europe and North Africa under the leadership of Colonel Benjamin O. Davis, Jr., a West Point graduate and son of the nation's only black general. Davis commanded the all-black 99th Pursuit Squadron which became a part of the 332nd Group. The 332nd won a Distinguished Unit Citation for its outstanding performance.

"Chappie" James was commissioned a second lieutenant in July of 1943. From then until the end of the war his main assignment was to train pilots for the 99th Pursuit Squadron. He had developed skill flying a variety of planes. His specialty was as a fighter pilot. It was in the Korean War that James first demonstrated his flying ability in combat. He flew 101 combat missions. He demonstrated his skill again in Vietnam when he flew 78 combat missions.

In the years between Korea and service in Vietnam, James had graduated from Air Command and Staff College at Maxwell Air Force Base in Alabama. He had been promoted and held important assignments in the United States and abroad. Upon his return from Vietnam, James was vice-commander of the 33rd Tactical Fighter Wing, Eglin Air Force Base in Florida. In 1969, he was promoted to the rank of brigadier general and named base commander of Wheelus Air Force Base in Libya.

The following year he became Deputy Assistant Secretary of Defense for Public Affairs, and was named major general while holding that post. In 1974, he became vice-commander of the Military Airlift Command at Scott Air Force Base in Illinois. One year later he became America's first black four-star general. (Benjamin O. Davis, Jr., was a lieutenant general when he retired.) At that time James became the commander of the North American Air Defense Command (NORAD), which meant that he was responsible for all aspects of the air defense of the United States and Canada. He remained in that command until health problems forced him to step down in December of 1977.

James played an important role throughout the 1960s and '70s when America was trying to resolve the discrepancies between the opportunities available to its black and white citizens. He was a living example of a black man who had made good. He was often asked to give talks on how he had overcome the hurdles he'd faced. He liked to tell young people— including his own children, Daniel, Claude, and Danice—the things he'd learned from his parents.

James's work had taken so much of his time and energy that he didn't get to spend a lot of time with his family. All through their marriage his wife had tried to get him to slow down. He had slowed down after he left NORAD, but he still had speaking engagements. One engagement was in Colorado the last week in February of 1978. Before leaving his wife, who was hospitalized with rheumatoid arthritis, they laughed and hugged and he told her he hoped she'd be feeling better by the time he got back.

After saying good-bye, "Chappie" James left for Colorado Springs. He had a heart attack and died there on February 25, 1978—just fourteen days after his fifty-eighth birthday. His body was flown back to Washington, D.C., where he was buried with the kind of honors usually reserved for presidents and other heads of state. More than 1,500 people attended his funeral. He was buried at Arlington National Cemetery.

In his relatively brief lifetime, "Chappie" James had dreamed what seemed to be an impossible dream—and he saw his dream come true.

"The Eagles Return to the Nest"
ॐ

CAST
Narrator
Six airmen

NARRATOR: This is a conversation that could have taken place in a hotel room in Tuskegee, Alabama, in August of 1977. The Tuskegee airmen—black military pilots who had been trained at Tuskegee Institute—were gathering for a great reunion the next day, which they called "The Eagles Return to the Nest." The six airmen came a day early and are sitting or standing around talking.

FIRST AIRMAN: (*opening a big brown envelope*) Do you ever hear from any of the other guys?

SECOND AIRMAN: Not directly, but I sure feel proud reading newspaper headlines like "William 'Bumps' Coleman Becomes Secretary of Transportation," "Elwood Driver Represents the U.S. Government in Airline Investigation," or "Coleman Young Elected Mayor of Detroit."

THIRD AIRMAN: (*watching with curiosity as the First Airman reaches into his envelope*) What do you have there?

FIRST AIRMAN: (*spreading pictures on the coffee table*) Some old pictures . . .

NARRATOR: The other men have been standing over by the window, but when they hear the word "pictures," they sit down on the couch or pull chairs up to the coffee table.

FOURTH AIRMAN: Let's see. (*picking up a picture*) Here's a picture of the legendary Wendell Pruitt. He and his crew were like a one-plane Air Force in World War II.

FIFTH AIRMAN: Don't forget "Lucky" Lester and "Buster" Hall when you're naming the all-time greats.

SIXTH AIRMAN: (*picking up the picture of a large group*) Here's a picture of all of us. We were a handsome bunch, weren't we?

FIRST AIRMAN: (*leaning forward to get a better look*) We sure were.

SECOND AIRMAN: (*after studying the picture for a while, he speaks in a sad tone.*) We really had high hopes when this picture was taken. We'd come home from the war as flying aces with big plans for careers in aviation.

THIRD AIRMAN: Yeah, I remember the day we met in Louisville to start Mercury Airlines.

FOURTH AIRMAN: But between segregation laws and big companies buying up all the transport planes, it was impossible for blacks to break into commercial flying at that time.

FIFTH AIRMAN: Some guys were able to keep flying, though. Jimmy Plenton and Perry Young set up an island-hopping service in the Caribbean. They eventually sold it. Jimmy Plenton and Hannibal Cox became vice presidents at Eastern Airlines.

SIXTH AIRMAN: Just think, they may be here tomorrow. Whoever thought up this reunion had a good idea. It'll sure be good to see all the guys again.

FIRST AIRMAN: It's been a long time.

SECOND AIRMAN: More than thirty years.

THIRD AIRMAN: Who all do you suppose will be coming?

FOURTH AIRMAN: It'll be interesting to see.

FIFTH AIRMAN: I understand that Larry Clark will be here. He's really worked hard to publicize the story of the Tuskegee airmen.

SIXTH AIRMAN: He and "Chappie" James were roommates, weren't they?

FIRST AIRMAN: Yeah. "Chappie" had finished the Civilian Pilot Training Program and had been a civilian instructor before he entered the military cadet program. So even though he was a student, everybody looked up to him.

SECOND AIRMAN: He was "Mr. Self-Confidence."

THIRD AIRMAN: But even "Chappie" couldn't have guessed that he'd be a four-star general and Commander in Chief of NORAD!

FOURTH AIRMAN: You're right about that. There was discrimination everywhere you turned in those days.

FIFTH AIRMAN: "Chappie" ran into his share of that, but he was one determined fellow. He would have been a leader in whatever kind of work he chose.

SIXTH AIRMAN: He was a go-getter, all right. I have never seen anybody with the determination he had. They said he was a no-nonsense instructor. He was an expert and he expected his students to become experts.

FIRST AIRMAN: But he liked to have fun, too. Remember how he used to fly low and buzz the girls' dorms? And how he used to be emcee at the talent shows?

SECOND AIRMAN: And do more singing and dancing than anybody else in the show?

THIRD AIRMAN: What I remember best is how "Chappie" could eat. I can see him now with a piece of possum in one hand and a slice of sweet potato pie in the other.

FOURTH AIRMAN: Yet, with all that, he was someone you could talk with if you had a problem.

FIFTH AIRMAN: He sure was.

SIXTH AIRMAN: I can't wait until tomorrow to see "Chappie" and all the others.

FIRST AIRMAN: Me too. I'm going to say good-night to you gentlemen now. Tomorrow's going to be quite a day!

CHARLES DREW

ALTHOUGH CHARLES DREW'S DREAM was to become a doctor, he was best known in high school and in college as an athlete. At Dunbar High School in Washington, D.C.—considered the best black high school in the nation at that time—he was a four-letter man in sports. He received the James E. Walker Memorial Medal for all-around athletic performance.

When Drew graduated from Amherst College in 1926, he was a star quarterback, the most valuable baseball player, captain of the track team, and national high hurdles champion. He received the Howard Hill Mossman Trophy as the man who had contributed the most to athletics during his four years at Amherst.

After college, Drew took a job as athletic director, football coach, and science instructor at Morgan State College in Baltimore. Under his leadership, Morgan basketball and football teams became championship teams. During this period Charles lived with his parents, Richard and Nora Drew, in Arlington, Virginia, commuting to Baltimore.

Charles Drew was born June 3, 1904, the oldest of five children in a close-knit family of modest means. Although sports

dominated his life, he held fast to his dream of becoming a doctor. He knew he would have to earn his own way, and saved all the money he could. In 1928, two years after finishing college, he entered medical school at McGill University in Montreal, Canada. He paid his school expenses with his savings, some borrowed money, and earnings from waiting on tables at the university.

Charles Drew excelled in sports at McGill, just as he had at Amherst and in high school. He won Canadian championships in track, setting an all-time high scoring record. Somehow, even though he worked and participated in sports, he earned higher grades than he had in college. In 1931, he received a scholarship which made it possible to spend more time on his studies. He was elected to the honorary scholastic fraternity, won the annual prize in neuroanatomy, and in his senior year was awarded the Williams Prize as tops in his graduating class.

While attending McGill, Drew joined Dr. John Beattie, a British professor, in doing blood research. He found it fascinating and decided to give further attention to it. During his two years at Montreal General Hospital—as an intern and resident doctor—he continued his research on blood.

Drew wanted very much to help prepare black students for medical careers. In 1935, he joined the faculty of Howard University's Medical School. The dean of the school wanted to build a first-rate medical faculty and Charles Drew received a fellowship for specialized advanced training. This made it possible for him to go to New York and study at Columbia University Medical School with Dr. John Scudder, who was doing blood research. Dr. Drew's assignment was to learn all he could about collecting and storing blood until it was needed for transfusions. He experimented with blood plasma and discovered that it could be used instead of whole blood. It lasted longer and was less likely to become contaminated. Dr. Drew published his findings in an article called "Banked Blood," since the process of collecting and storing blood was called "banking" it.

During his studies, Charles Drew had the assistance and support of his wife, Lenore, a former teacher in Atlanta. She learned laboratory techniques and helped him with his work.

It was 1940 when Dr. Drew earned his Doctor of Medical Science degree from Columbia University. World War II had started in Europe. Drew and other American blood specialists were exploring ways to get life-saving blood plasma to the war front when Charles received an urgent request from his former teacher, Dr. John Beattie, who had returned to England. A cablegram asked for 5,000 ampules of dried plasma for transfusions, plus the same amount three weeks later. Being an excellent organizer, Dr. Drew went into action immediately. He was chosen medical supervisor of the "Blood for Britain" project, which helped save the lives of many wounded soldiers.

Following this success, Charles Drew was named director of the Red Cross Blood Bank and assistant director of the National Research Council, in charge of blood collection for the U.S. Army and Navy. As Drew set up the blood bank and trained the staff, he felt he just had to speak out against the armed forces' directive to the Red Cross: that blood was to be separated according to the race of the donor. Dr. Drew knew this was wrong, that there was no racial difference in blood. Soldiers and sailors would die needlessly if they had to wait for "same race" blood. At that time it was common practice for leading medical experts to be commissioned in the armed forces, but Dr. Drew was not. Friends who knew him wondered if this was because of his objection to segregated blood.

In 1944, Charles Drew was awarded the Spingarn Medal of the National Association for the Advancement of Colored People for his contributions to science. He was still interested in training young black doctors and helping them get established successfully. He didn't want racial discrimination to separate doctors from people who needed their help. He returned to Howard University in Washington, D.C., as head of surgery. In addition to his work there, he was a consultant for many hospitals and medical schools and in great demand as a speaker. Often he had a long, strenuous day before setting out for his speaking engagements. This was the case on April 1, 1950.

The previous day he performed several operations and then attended a student banquet in the evening. Dr. Drew was to deliver the annual lecture at the Andrew Memorial Clinic in Tuskegee, Alabama. Some students and colleagues wanted to attend and asked Dr. Drew to drive them there. After only a few hours rest, he and his passengers started out for Alabama. Near Burlington, North Carolina, Dr. Drew dozed off as he drove. The car ran off the road and turned over. Drew was badly injured.

Newspaper accounts said that the hospital nearest the accident refused to admit Dr. Drew because of his race, and that precious time was lost in taking him farther down the road to a black hospital. By the time he arrived there, he had lost so much blood that no one could have saved his life. It seemed a cruel hoax that the man who had done more than anyone else in the world to make blood transfusions available to people in emergency situations did not have access to a blood transfusion when he needed it.

Thousands of people filed past Dr. Charles Drew's casket at his funeral, and thousands more sent messages expressing their sympathy to his family. His accomplishments were recognized and appreciated.

Who Was Dr. Charles Drew?

❧

CAST

New Child	Third Child
Old Child	Fourth Child
Mrs. Mauldin	Fifth Child
Dr. Smith	Sixth Child
Narrator	

The part of the New Child can be played by a boy or a girl. Whoever plays the part can use his or her own name in the script. The Old Child is not really an "old" child but one who has been going to Drew School all the time. The part can be played by a boy or a girl, and his or her own name can be used.

SCENE 1

NARRATOR: A new student knocks on the door of Mrs. Mauldin's fifth-grade classroom. Mrs. Mauldin goes to the door and greets the child.

MRS. MAULDIN: Hello! Welcome to Room 7. (*speaking to the class*) Class, I'd like you to meet your new classmate whose name is _____.

MRS. MAULDIN: (*to New Child*) Here's a desk next to _____. (*uses name of person playing Old Child*)

MRS. MAULDIN: (*to Old Child*) _____, please show _____ around.

OLD CHILD: (*to New Child*) Hi! Do you want to take a walk around the school?

NEW CHILD: OK. Thanks.

OLD CHILD: Let's go. (*They go out into the hall.*)

SCENE 2

OLD CHILD: These are all classrooms, and down there is the office.

NEW CHILD: Whose picture is that hanging up on the wall?

OLD CHILD: Oh, that's Charles Drew, the man this school is named for.

NEW CHILD: Why? What did he do?

OLD CHILD: He made it so that if somebody's in an accident or needs an operation, they can have a blood transfusion.

NEW CHILD: Really?

OLD CHILD: Yeah. Thanks to his blood transfusions, a whole lot of soldiers came out of the war alive.

NEW CHILD: Yeah? What war was that?

OLD CHILD: I don't remember. Ask Mrs. Mauldin. She told us once, but I forget.

NARRATOR: Old Child looks at the clock.

OLD CHILD: Oh, it's time to get back to the room.

SCENE 3

NARRATOR: It is the end of the day and the teacher speaks to the New Child.

MRS. MAULDIN: Hope you had a good day. Do you think you'll like Drew School?

NEW CHILD: I think so. When I can make some friends, I think it'll be OK. Mrs. Mauldin, can I ask you something?

MRS. MAULDIN: (*wondering what the child will say*) Yes, of course.

NEW CHILD: In what war did Charles Drew save all those soldiers' lives?

MRS. MAULDIN: It was World War II. He didn't go in person to save their lives, but he discovered that blood plasma could be stored and then used for blood transfusions when soldiers were hurt in battle.

NEW CHILD: I see. I never knew about him before.

MRS. MAULDIN: You know, you've just reminded me of something I've been intending to do.

NEW CHILD: What's that?

MRS. MAULDIN: Well, my next-door neighbor is a retired doctor who used to be a student of Dr. Drew's. I invite him to come talk to my class each year, but haven't set up a date for this year yet.

NEW CHILD: I'm glad you waited until I came.

MRS. MAULDIN: So am I. See you tomorrow.

SCENE 4

NARRATOR: Dr. Smith has come to speak to Mrs. Mauldin's class. Dr. Smith and Mrs. Mauldin are standing in the front of the classroom. The children are all sitting on the floor in front of them.

MRS. MAULDIN: Class, I'd like you to meet Dr. Smith. He's my next-door neighbor, but more importantly, he is a surgeon who studied with Dr. Charles Drew for whom our school is named.

DR. SMITH: Hello, class. At one time Dr. Drew was my teacher. I was older than you are now. It was after I'd finished college and was in medical school at Howard University in Washington, D.C.

OLD CHILD: Did Dr. Drew look like that picture out in the hall?

DR. SMITH: Yes, he did. He was about six feet tall. Very well-built. Very athletic. Did you know that he excelled in football, baseball, and track?

THIRD CHILD: No!

DR. SMITH: He won his first sports event as a swimmer when he was only nine years old. He went on to star in sports all through high school, college, and medical school. He won championships in the United States and Canada . . .

FOURTH CHILD: (*blurts out*) Canada? I thought you knew Dr. Drew in Washington. Why was he in Canada?

DR. SMITH: He went to medical school in Montreal, Canada. That's where he got interested in blood chemistry.

FIFTH CHILD: How did Dr. Drew get from Canada to the second World War?

DR. SMITH: After Montreal he went to Howard University. Then he got a scholarship for more study in New York. Doctors there were trying to find ways to save blood for emergency use. But they were using whole blood. Dr. Drew discovered that blood plasma would work.

SIXTH CHILD: Had the war started?

DR. SMITH: Yes, and word came that British soldiers needed lots of blood plasma. Dr. Drew was chosen to organize a "Blood for Britain" project.

NEW CHILD: Wow, he was really a war hero!

DR. SMITH: Yes, I guess he was. But Dr. Drew did something even more important. He was also in charge of blood collection for the U.S. Army and Navy during the war. The Red Cross said that blood was to be separated according to the race of the donor. Dr. Drew knew this was wrong. There is no racial difference in blood, and he spoke out against separating blood from whites and blood from blacks.

THIRD CHILD: Did people believe him?

DR. SMITH: It took a long time, but finally they did.

FOURTH CHILD: What did Dr. Drew do next?

DR. SMITH: Well, I'm happy to say he went back to Howard University to teach, because that's when I got a chance to be in his class.

FIFTH CHILD: What was he like?

DR. SMITH: He was caring and considerate. No matter how busy he was, he had time for you. He helped his students get jobs. He worked hard to get equal opportunities for black surgeons.

MRS. MAULDIN: Class, I think our time is about up. Dr. Smith, thank you so much for coming today. I know we have all enjoyed finding out about Dr. Drew.

NARRATOR: Old Child raises his (*or her*) hand.

OLD CHILD: I just want to say that from now on, every time I pass that picture in the hall I'm going to remember what you have told us.

NEW CHILD: I'm sure glad I came to this school.

FREDERICK DOUGLASS

IF YOU WALK UP TO THE Frederick Douglass home in Anacostia, you feel as if the noted Abolitionist-orator-editor-statesman might step out to greet you. The home is a mansion on a hill across the Potomac River from the heart of Washington, D.C. It is as different as night and day from the place where Frederick Douglass was born.

Frederick Douglass began life as Frederick Bailey, a slave child who was born in a tiny cabin on a Maryland plantation. He barely knew his mother—whose first name was Harriet—because she lived and worked on a different plantation. She died when he was very young. But the few times he saw her helped him figure out his probable birthday. She called him "her Valentine," so he celebrated his birthday on February 14. He never knew for sure, but believed that the slaveholder was his father, and that 1817 was the year of his birth.

As a little boy, Frederick ran errands on the plantation and was a playmate of the master's son. But he and the other slave children were sometimes whipped and often went hungry. Many a night they had to fight the dogs for scraps of food.

When Frederick was about nine years old, he was sent to

his master's relatives in Baltimore to be a houseboy for Mrs. Sophia Auld. Although he was still a slave, he found that life in the city was not as harsh as it was on the plantation. He was also fortunate in that Mrs. Auld decided to teach him to read. This went against her husband's wishes. When her husband found that his wife was teaching Frederick, he ordered her to stop at once. Slaveholders didn't want slaves to have schooling, because they thought that if slaves ever read about freedom, they'd want it for themselves.

Frederick's reading lessons stopped, but his desire to learn continued. He kept his spelling book tucked inside his shirt, and studied it every time he got a chance. With some money he earned shining shoes, he bought a book, *The Columbian Orator*. That book included speeches by great men, many of them about liberty and freedom. Frederick read it over and over. And just as his master feared, Frederick was no longer content to be a slave.

Before he could run away, young Douglass was sent back to his old plantation. There he was hired out to a "slave breaker," a man who worked slaves exceedingly hard and tried to beat them into submission. Frederick was in his late teens by this time. He was flogged endlessly, but he did not let it break his spirit. It made him all the more eager to be free.

He tried to escape, forging passes for himself and four other slaves. Local slaveholders threatened to shoot him on sight. He was considered a "dangerous Negro," and his master sent him away—back to Baltimore—and hired him out to work in the shipyards there. White workers objected to blacks working with them, and again Frederick suffered beatings. Eventually, with the help of some black freedmen and his future wife, he managed to escape from slave territory and arrived in New York. He was twenty-one years old when he first set foot on free soil.

While in Baltimore, Douglass had met and fallen in love with a free black woman named Anna Murray. She joined him in New York, and they were married in the home of David Ruggles, a black Abolitionist. Frederick had read newspapers and knew about white people in America who did not believe in slavery. They were called Abolitionists. He wanted to find out more about them.

Soon afterward, the couple moved to Massachusetts. It was there that Frederick took the last name, Douglass, and dropped his slave name, Bailey. Although slavery was prohibited in Massachusetts, there was still racial prejudice. But there was also a great deal of anti-slavery feeling. Frederick Douglass became a black Abolitionist, and soon was one of their most forceful and convincing orators. In 1841, he spoke at an Anti-Slavery Society meeting in Nantucket. People were moved by what he had to say, and they believed him. The Society hired him as an agent to help promote their work.

Douglass spoke throughout the North. Important people of the time were impressed. He was such a good speaker that some listeners questioned whether he had actually been a slave. In an effort to prove he was, he wrote his life story, giving specific details and the names of people and places. Before long, his old slave master was attempting to reclaim his "property." Fearing capture as a fugitive slave, Douglass went to England. There, friends raised money to purchase his freedom.

When he returned to America in 1847, Douglass started a newspaper, *The North Star*, in Rochester, New York. There, he and his family aided slaves escaping to freedom in Canada.

Frederick Douglass also continued his anti-slavery activities. He made more speeches. He spoke out against prejudice and job discrimination. He was a friend of John Brown. He tried to talk Brown out of the famous attack on Harper's Ferry in West Virginia in which Brown hoped to get slaves to rise up against their owners. Even so, slaveowners accused Douglass

of supporting the raid. He fled to Canada and from there went to England again in order to avoid any action they might take.

When the Civil War broke out, Douglass was back in this country. He saw the war as a chance for black men to fight for their freedom. He urged President Abraham Lincoln to enlist black troops, and eventually Lincoln followed his advice. More than 200,000 black servicemen signed up, including Douglass' own sons.

After the war, Douglass worked to get full rights of citizenship for former slaves. They were freed by the Emancipation Proclamation of 1863, but still faced many hardships. He and his family moved to Washington, D.C. He was made a United States Marshall, and later the Recorder of Deeds for the District of Columbia. In 1889, he was appointed Minister to Haiti.

Frederick Douglass returned to the United States in 1891. He continued to write and do some speaking to the very end of his life. On the day of his death, February 20, 1895, he had spoken to the National Council of Women. Many years before, he had defended the right of women to vote at the first women's rights meeting in Seneca Falls, New York.

Douglass received many honors during his lifetime. In the years since his death, there have been many tributes also. A commemorative postage stamp was issued, a bridge in Washington was named for him, and the federal government purchased his Anacostia home, so that the American public can visit it.

The Douglass "Station" of the Underground Railroad

&

CAST

Frederick Douglass	First son
Anna Douglass	Second son
Harriet Tubman	First Narrator
Eight fugitive slaves	Second Narrator

FIRST NARRATOR: It is late one night in early November, sometime after the 1850 Fugitive Slave Act has become law. Harriet Tubman and a party of eight fugitive slaves have just arrived outside the Douglass home in Rochester, New York.

SECOND NARRATOR: Harriet Tubman goes from a wooded area to the back door, trying to stay in the shadows of the house. Her knock is so quiet it can hardly be heard.

HARRIET: (*Knock, knock. Pause. Knock, knock.*)

FIRST NARRATOR: One of Douglass' sons looks out the window and whispers:

FIRST SON: It's Moses.

SECOND NARRATOR: Frederick Douglass turns the lamplight off and goes to the door—just barely opening it.

FREDERICK DOUGLASS: Come in, Moses.

FIRST NARRATOR: Harriet Tubman steps inside, and whispers . . .

HARRIET TUBMAN: I have eight. I had them wait in the woods 'til I knew it was safe to come in.

FREDERICK DOUGLASS: One of my sons is the lookout. He let us know you were nearby and that the coast is clear.

ANNA DOUGLASS: Welcome, Harriet. Have them come in.

SECOND NARRATOR: Harriet Tubman signals to her company of slaves. One at a time they approach the house just as she had done.

FIRST NARRATOR: Douglass barely opens the door and admits the slaves. Once they are inside, they gather near the fireplace to warm themselves after their long journey. Some are barefooted; others are wearing summer-weight clothes.

SECOND NARRATOR: Douglass silently shakes hands with the fugitives, then in a low voice says,

FREDERICK DOUGLASS: Congratulations. Moses has brought you to the doorstep of freedom. The land of Canada is just across the lake. You'll be there by this time tomorrow night.

ANNA DOUGLASS: Meanwhile, here's food and some blankets so you can eat and then rest.

FIRST NARRATOR: She gestures to an iron pot in the fireplace and blankets in the corner.

FREDERICK DOUGLASS: I know from experience what it's like to escape. You really can't relax until you get to the Promised Land.

SECOND NARRATOR: The Douglass' second son appears at the door with a huge ladle and dishes up stew for everyone. In the meantime the first son has gone to take his turn as the lookout.

ANNA DOUGLASS to HARRIET TUBMAN: How was your trip?

HARRIET TUBMAN: (*eating like she's really hungry, but in a hurry to get through—talks between mouthfuls*) We had lots of close calls, but made it safely this far. Main thing was trying to race the snow. Didn't want that to catch us. Can't take the chance of leaving tracks.

FREDERICK DOUGLASS to HARRIET TUBMAN: Which route did you take this time?

HARRIET TUBMAN: (*obviously worried about something as she talks*) Eastern Shore to Wilmington in Delaware. Some of the young ones got scared when they heard the slave catchers' dogs. We had to wade in water so the dogs would lose our scent.

FREDERICK DOUGLASS: It must have been a relief to reach Thomas Garrett's house in Wilmington, wasn't it?

HARRIET TUBMAN: (*trying to answer Douglass' question, although it is more and more obvious she has something else on her mind*) Yes, he gave us dry clothes and we slept a while. He had a former friend take us to Philadelphia in a wagon with a false bottom.

FREDERICK DOUGLASS: Where William Still met you—right?

HARRIET TUBMAN: Yes. (*then, putting her dish down abruptly*) Excuse me, Frederick, but what's the plan for us going from here to Canada?

FREDERICK DOUGLASS: I've arranged for a friend to get you and your party on the morning train. You'll have to board before daylight, so you won't be seen. Hope you don't mind having to travel in the baggage car. It's getting harder and harder to cross the border.

HARRIET TUBMAN: Let me stop you, Frederick. I thank you for what you're planning, but I won't feel safe 'til we get on the Canadian side. Can you possibly get somebody to take us across the lake tonight? All of a sudden I had this strange feeling the slave catchers are on our trail.

ANNA DOUGLASS: Can't you wait until morning? As tired as you all are, a good night's sleep would do you some good.

HARRIET TUBMAN: Thank you, Anna. I am bone tired and the others are too, but I can't chance waiting. Morning may be too late.

FREDERICK DOUGLASS: What makes you so sure slave catchers are trailing you?

HARRIET TUBMAN: There's a $40,000 reward on my head and lots of people want to cash in. I don't know what gave me this feeling, but my hunches have been right too many times before to ignore them.

FIRST NARRATOR: Douglass' second son has made an inconspicuous exit while his parents talked with Harriet Tubman. That son now reappears and announces,

SECOND SON: Excuse me for interrupting, but my brother and I have arranged to take you across the lake.

HARRIET TUBMAN: Oh, thank you. (*turning to Frederick and Anna*) You certainly raised your sons well. Thank you all!

SECOND NARRATOR: Harriet gathers her things and wakens the fugitives in her group.

HARRIET TUBMAN: Hurry now. It's time to go.

FREDERICK DOUGLASS: (*shaking Harriet's hand*) Have a safe journey, Moses.

ANNA DOUGLASS: (*giving Harriet a hug*) God be with you.

FIRST SON: (*in an urgent whisper*) The coast is clear. Let's go.

FIRST NARRATOR: Harriet and the fugitives walk in the shadows as the Douglass' first son leads the way to the shores of Lake Ontario.

SECOND NARRATOR: There the second son is waiting to help them into a boat and they all set out for the Canadian shore.

IDA B. WELLS

SOMETIMES IT SEEMS THAT one lone person can't do much to change the world around them. Ida B. Wells is proof that one person *can* make a big difference. Ida spent most of her life overcoming one huge obstacle after another—because she cared about others.

Ida was born to slave parents during the Civil War—the eldest child in a large family. The date was July 16, 1862, and the place was Holly Springs, Mississippi. Ida's mother, Elizabeth, had been sold away from her family in Virginia when she was a little girl. She was cook on the Bolling plantation. It was there that she met and married James Wells. James Wells was his master's son and had been sent to the plantation in Holly Springs to learn the carpenter's trade.

When slavery ended, James and Elizabeth both continued to work for Mr. Bolling, but now he paid them for the work they did. The end of slavery also meant the beginning of a chance for education for blacks. James and Elizabeth wanted to learn all they could, and to have their children enjoy the educational opportunities they had been denied.

When a school was started in Holly Springs, Ida and her

mother enrolled. Ida's father had managed to learn a little about reading, but did not know enough to read about all the things he was interested in. Ida became the person in the family who could read best. As she grew up, her father would ask her to read the newspaper to groups of his friends.

In 1870, the Fifteenth Amendment to the Constitution gave black men the right to vote. (No women were allowed to vote until many years later.) Ida's father and his friends cherished this privilege. They wanted to be well-informed about politics. But politics made a change for the Wells family. Mr. Bolling wanted James Wells to vote one way, and he wanted to vote another way—and did. After the election, Mr. Bolling dismissed James Wells from the carpenter shop. He and Elizabeth "retired" from work on the Bolling plantation. He opened his own carpentry shop, and she changed employers.

Ida's life took a turn when she was sixteen years old. She'd gone to visit her grandmother's farm. Being there, she didn't know that a yellow fever epidemic had struck her hometown, until men on horseback came to tell her that both her parents had died. She rushed back to town to see about her brothers and sisters. Her father's friends offered to take some of the children into their homes, but Ida did not want the family separated. Her parents had left them a house to live in, and she figured she could get a teaching job. Ida had read every book in the library, and was able to teach in a rural area.

She got a teaching job about six miles from home. (She combed her hair in a more grown-up style and wore a long dress, so she would look older than she really was.) Each Sunday Ida rode into the country on a big white mule. She lived with her students' families during the week, returning home on the mule for weekends. Once there, she cooked, washed, and ironed for the next week. Her grandmother or a neighbor stayed with the children when Ida was away.

After two years, Ida's Aunt Fannie invited her to come to Memphis and offered to take in two of her sisters and raise them with her own children. Her husband had died in the yellow fever epidemic. Another aunt agreed to take Ida's sister Eugenia, who was paralyzed and needed special care, and the two brothers. This aunt had a farm and was glad to have the boys help her.

Ida found a teaching job in Woodstock, a town ten miles from Memphis. She could take a train back and forth. During summer vacation she took courses at Fisk University and Lemoyne Institute, so that she would be qualified to teach in the Memphis schools. She liked the city, with its concerts, plays, and lectures. She met new people, and took pride in seeing successful black-owned businesses.

There were some disturbing things happening, though. One was an incident on the train Ida took. She was in the ladies coach, as usual, reading a book. When the conductor came to collect tickets, he refused to accept hers. He told her to move to the segregated "Jim Crow" coach for blacks. She refused to move and was pushed off the train at the next station.

Ida took action. She had faith in the justice system, and sued and won her cause in circuit court. Feeling that justice had been done, she wrote a newspaper article about the incident. (Later, she was disappointed when the decision was overturned by the Tennessee Supreme Court.)

Ida was asked to write more articles for a number of black newspapers. She wrote about problems she cared about—the poor quality of education in the Memphis schools, how things were getting more and more difficult for black people in the South. She used a pen name, but her identity was known, and Ida Wells was dismissed from her teaching job.

Then something tragic happened. Three black men were lynched—murdered. One was a close friend of Ida's. He and his partners in a successful black grocery store were killed by people who wanted to force them out of business. Ida wrote articles demanding the arrest and conviction of the guilty parties. This was the beginning of her crusade to stop lynching. She wrote and traveled and gave lectures.

Her campaign was not popular with a lot of people, but T. Thomas Fortune, editor of the newspaper *New York Age* in New York City, knew of Ida B. Wells and supported her crusade. He asked her to write articles for his paper. Ida went to New York and was in great demand as a lecturer. The Women's Loyal League, an organization of black women in New York, paid her way to England where she helped found a British group against lynching.

Back home she found new problems. The World's Columbian Exposition in Chicago in 1893 was ignoring the contributions of black people—people like Crispus Attucks, the first American to give his life in the Revolution; Benjamin Banneker, who made the first American clock; Granville Woods, who invented railroad telegraphy. Ida had to speak out. She and her husband-to-be, Ferdinand Lee Barnett, distributed a pamphlet to protest this omission.

Barnett shared Ida's social concerns. He was founder of the first black newspaper in Illinois. The two were married on June 27, 1895. They had four children: Charles, Herman, Ida, and Alfreda. When the children were young, Ida did less traveling and speaking, but soon she was as active as ever. She turned her attention to the many southern blacks who were moving to northern cities to escape the situation in the South and to find work. She wanted to help these people and their families. She started a kindergarten, helped set up a dormitory and job placement center. She and her husband knew that many people needed legal assistance and did not know how to get it. From 1913 to 1916, Ida Wells was a probation officer for the Chicago Municipal Court.

Ida urged other women to become more active in community, city, and national activities to improve conditions for themselves and their families. She organized women in Chicago. Many such black women's clubs were started in other cities across the country. Eventually, these groups merged to form the National Association of Colored Women's Clubs. The new organization was sometimes referred to by its initials NACW. Ida became chairwoman of the resolutions committee and an old friend of hers, Mary Church Terrell, whom Ida had met years before in Memphis, became president.

Ida and Mary were the only two women who took part in a meeting to set up the National Association for the Advancement of Colored People, the NAACP. They both worked with Jane Addams, the social worker. They appealed to the President of the United States to enlist help in guaranteeing the rights of full citizenship to all Americans. Both were active in the women's rights suffrage movement. They believed that both men and women should have the right to vote.

Ida B. Wells died in Chicago on March 25, 1931. This one woman had changed many things in the world around her.

The Beauty of Being Free

❧

CAST

Ida B. Wells as a child   Second Narrator

Mr. Wells   Six other men who are Mr.

First Narrator   Wells' friends

The newspaper that Ida reads from can be any newspaper. She should pretend that it has the story about Hiram Revels.

FIRST NARRATOR: Newly emancipated slaves realized that to be able to read is the most precious gift of all.

SECOND NARRATOR: Having been denied the chance to learn during slavery days, they got busy learning as soon as they had the chance.

FIRST NARRATOR: After the war, the Freedmen's Bureau and some church groups started schools. These schools weren't all inside buildings. Sometimes people just gathered in the shade of a big old tree.

SECOND NARRATOR: Wherever the school was, former slaves came to it from miles around. Nobody thought they were too old, or felt shy if they couldn't read as good as they wanted to. They just practiced until they got better.

FIRST NARRATOR: Ida B. Wells and her mother went to school together. Mrs. Wells had to go to work, and take care of Ida and her brothers and sisters, so she couldn't spend all her time reading.

SECOND NARRATOR: But young Ida could—and she did.

FIRST NARRATOR: She read everything and really got good at it.

SECOND NARRATOR: Mr. Wells could read a little bit, but he was anxious to get information in newspapers that were hard to read.

FIRST NARRATOR: So he used to have Ida sit up on a stool and read to him and his friends.

SECOND NARRATOR: The year is 1874.

FIRST NARRATOR: The place is Mr. Wells' carpentry shop. It's nighttime and oil lamps light the room. Twelve-year-old Ida is sitting on a stool in the middle of the room. Her father and his friends are seated around her, listening intently as she reads.

IDA: (*has a newspaper with an article about former U.S. Senator Hiram Revels*) The headline says FORMER U.S. SENATOR HIRAM REVELS BECOMES PRESIDING ELDER OF THE HOLLY SPRINGS DISTRICT.

SECOND NARRATOR: Ida glances up from the paper, then reads on.

IDA: The Honorable Hiram Revels, the first black Senator in the United States Congress, has been named Presiding Elder of the Methodist Episcopal Church. He will make his home in Holly Springs, Mississippi. In addition to performing his duties as Presiding Elder, Senator Revels has been appointed to the Rust College faculty. He is the former president of Alcorn College.

MR. WELLS: Hum, I knew he was going to be Presiding Elder, but I didn't know he was going to teach at Rust. (*turning to Ida*) Ida, if you are patient, you may have a Senator for a teacher some-day, since you're in the grade school at Rust.

IDA: Oh, I hope so!

FIRST MAN: I will never forget February 25, 1870. That was the day Hiram Revels became Senator.

SECOND MAN: Yes, indeed. I wish I could have been in Washington, D.C., that day!

THIRD MAN: That would have been the best place to see it, but the newspapers told about it pretty good. They said people started to the Capitol before day and by noon you couldn't get a seat. People knew this was the day of decision, and they came from far and wide to see history made.

FOURTH MAN: They sure did. Remember that Senator who got up there and said, "I would avert if possible this great, great ca-lamity."

FIFTH MAN: But then another one—I think his name was Senator Cameron from Pennsylvania, if I remember rightly—said Ne-groes were citizens by a higher law, that of having fought for and helped save the Union!

SIXTH MAN: Senator Sumner from Massachusetts was another one that spoke up for Revels.

MR. WELLS: In the meantime, Revels sat in the lounge patiently waiting. He knew he had been elected fair and square, and he had faith that everything would work itself out. You know how he has a way of raring back in his chair? I can picture him sitting like that all during the wait.

FIRST MAN: I will never forget those pictures when the Senate finally voted 48 to 8, and when he walked with dignity down the aisle.

SECOND MAN: Yes, indeed. That was a proud moment for us all— even if we weren't able to see it with our own eyes.

THIRD MAN: But I can still close my eyes and imagine how it must have been.

FIRST NARRATOR: Ida closes her eyes as she listens. The Third Man continues.

THIRD MAN: The people in the galleries all stood and clapped.

FOURTH MAN: They sure did. Remember the paper said, "It was exactly 4:40 P.M. when Senator Hiram Revels was sworn in."

FIFTH MAN: If you ask me, I think Revels could have pressed harder for our rights.

SIXTH MAN: He did quite a bit. You've got to remember, he voted to enforce the Fifteenth Amendment and for naturalization for colored people.

IDA: (*who has been daydreaming as she listens to every word*) I hope I can go to Congress one day.

MR. WELLS: I hope so, too, Ida. I've seen a lot of changes in my life. Why, ten years ago we were in slavery. Not one of us could have imagined my good friend James Hill would get to be Secretary of State for Mississippi. And he's as good a man as ever held that job.

FIRST MAN: I will never forget four years ago when we first got the vote.

SECOND MAN: Yes, indeed, we had waited a long, long time for that.

IDA: You know what I wish? That women could vote, too. It doesn't seem fair that men can vote, but women are not allowed to vote.

MR. WELLS: You have a point there, Ida.

THIRD MAN: But I'm afraid it's going to take a lot more years before you talk Congress into that. They went around and around on that Fifteenth Amendment.

FOURTH MAN: They sure did. Remember how they tried to have a "grandfather clause"?

IDA: A grandfather clause? What's that?

MR. WELLS: It was a rule that your grandfather had to have been able to vote before the Civil War. That left out most colored people if their grandfathers were slaves.

FIFTH MAN: I think we'll see changes, though, and (*turning to Ida*) one day you'll be able to vote.

SIXTH MAN: (*realizing how late it has gotten*) I think I'd better be going. I have a long day tomorrow.

MR. WELLS: But isn't it wonderful to know that nowadays when you put in a long day you'll get paid for it?

SECOND NARRATOR: The men get up to leave after saying "Goodnight" to Mr. Wells and Ida.

FIRST NARRATOR: As Ida folded up her newspaper, she thought back on the evening. She had the opportunity to learn to read better than her father or any of his friends. It seemed so unfair that such intelligent men would have to have a child read to them. Yet it didn't keep them from being interested and informed. She had learned so much from them. She hoped that someday everybody would have an opportunity to learn reading. Then, daydreaming again, she thought that maybe she would write for a newspaper when she grew up. That would make her father and his friends real proud.

OSCAR MICHEAUX

WHEN OSCAR MICHEAUX WAS A little boy on his father's farm in southern Illinois, little did he—or anyone else—dream that he would become the most prolific black American movie producer of all time. In the years between 1918 and 1948, he wrote, directed, produced, and distributed from 34 to 45 motion pictures. His company made the first full-length films with casts of black actors and actresses.

Micheaux's films showed black people in a variety of roles. Hollywood was limiting black actors and actresses to parts as southern maids, butlers, farmers—only supporting roles. Micheaux cast black people as heroes, heroines, good guys, bad guys, and everything in-between. He was the first film maker to show black people as pioneers in the West.

Micheaux knew about life as a pioneer. He had homesteaded on land he had purchased near the Rosebud Indian Reservation in South Dakota. He learned the hard way, but succeeded and became a wealthy man by the time he was in his early twenties. He decided to write a novel about his many unusual experiences as the only black homesteader within hundreds of miles. His book was illustrated and sold for $1.50. He eventually wrote six more novels.

It was Micheaux's work as a novelist that led to his career as a film maker. Another black film maker, George Johnson, had heard of one of Micheaux's books and asked to buy the movie rights. He and Micheaux talked, but couldn't agree on terms, so Micheaux decided to film the story himself. This was typical of Micheaux's style. After he finished his first novel, he wasn't able to find a publisher, so he established his own publishing company. He was a supersalesman with a flair for showmanship. On publication of a book, he would load copies in his car and go on an extensive tour—promoting and selling the book on farms, in city schools, churches, and homes, wherever he could interest people in buying it.

Oscar Micheaux was born on January 2, 1884, on a farm near Cairo, Illinois. He was one of thirteen children born to Calvin and Belle Micheaux, both of whom were former slaves. The family later moved to the town of Metropolis, Illinois, so that the children could attend public school there.

When Oscar was about fourteen, the family moved back to the farm. He didn't show much interest in farming, but did take over the family marketing. He readily took an interest in how business was conducted.

At age seventeen, Oscar left the farm and headed west, working at odd jobs along the way. Eventually he got a job as a Pullman porter on trains which operated out of Chicago. Soon he was on a regular run between Chicago and Portland, Oregon. He had a chance to see the western part of the United States, and to save $2,340. He decided he wanted to settle in the West and used his money to buy the homesteading land in South Dakota. He constructed a sod house, plowed the land, bought horses, and went in for farming. By the time he was twenty-five, his land and his stock were valued at $20,000.

After a brief and unhappy marriage, Micheaux took comfort in reading. He read a book by Jack London in which London said that the way to write was simply to get a pencil and a piece of paper and start writing—and keep on until one had written something that someone else would want to read.

That's exactly what Micheaux did. He sat down and wrote, then published *Conquest*, the first of his seven novels. *The Homesteader* was the title of the novel that George Johnson of the Lincoln Motion Picture Company offered to buy. Motion pictures were relatively new, and had captured the imagination of the public. Micheaux was most interested in signing a movie contract, providing he could personally direct the film. George Johnson said, "No." Micheaux—never discouraged— organized his own film company. He went back to the midwestern farmers who had bought books from him. This time he sold them shares of stock in his film company. Soon he had enough money to produce an eight-reel movie version of *The Homesteader*.

That was in 1919, shortly after Hollywood had become the center of film production. For the next twenty-nine years— through the silent film era and well in the "talkies"—Oscar Micheaux produced movies featuring all black actors and actresses. Although self-taught, he supervised filming, handled the bookkeeping and distribution, in addition to writing the screen plays. At one point one of his brothers assisted him.

Being a black producer, Micheaux didn't have access to the training, equipment, or bookings that Hollywood producers had, but he made maximum use of the resources available to him. If he visited a home with an interesting entrance or staircase, he would ask to use it as a movie set. This saved the cost of using studios and provided a variety of settings. Similarly, if he was struck by a person's mannerisms or the way light fell across their face, he'd sign them up, even if he'd never met them before. That's how Lorenzo Tucker became "the black Valentino." Micheaux happened to see him sitting in a hotel lobby in Philadelphia, and before long had convinced Tucker that he had a promising future in films. Tucker acted in fourteen Micheaux productions. Micheaux signed up other stars—singer Paul Robeson and aviator Hubert Julian—because they were already known to the public.

Micheaux was equally resourceful when it came to raising money for his productions. As soon as he completed a film he would take scenes from it to black theater owners and to white theater owners who catered to black audiences. He was not only a supersalesman but his physical presence demanded attention. He was six feet tall and weighed 300 pounds. He wore long Russian coats and extravagant wide-brimmed hats. Often he would promote his new film and its stars so successfully that he was able to get bookings for the new movie and financial backing for his next film.

Some of Micheaux's films were controversial and drew criticism in the press, but that did not disturb him. It is impossible to give an accurate count of all his movies, since most have been lost or the film deteriorated. There were at least 34, perhaps as many as 45.

Oscar Micheaux was on one of his many promotional trips when he died in Charlotte, North Carolina, on April 1, 1951. He was sixty-seven years old. Considering his limited education, his limited funds, and the times in which he lived, he was quite remarkable. He entered the film industry when it was new and single-handedly explored its many possibilities. He not only opened the door for today's black actors, actresses, directors, producers, and screenwriters, he gave the world a broader view of black life.

Oscar Micheaux's Visit

❧

CAST

Helen, a student

Miss Mason, a visitor at school

Some children can pretend to be the teacher and parents who have come to hear the program. The rest of the class can pretend to be students who are listening to Helen and Miss Mason.

HELEN: *(to audience)* It's Grandparents' Day at school and the grandparents are telling our class about their childhood memories. My own grandma doesn't live close enough to visit, so I asked a neighbor if she would be my grandmother for the day. Now I'm going to interview her. You may be surprised at what she has to tell us.

HELEN: *(to Miss Mason)* Hello, Miss Mason, welcome to our class.

MISS MASON: Hello, Helen. Thank you for inviting me to come.

HELEN: Miss Mason, what is your most unforgettable childhood memory?

MISS MASON: I think it was when movie maker Oscar Micheaux came to our house.

HELEN: You mean he just came and rang the doorbell one day?

MISS MASON: No—he made a special trip to our house.

HELEN: Why? How come he did that?

MISS MASON: Well, my father used to own a movie theater . . .

HELEN: He did?

MISS MASON: (continuing) . . . and Oscar Micheaux would bring his films and stay at our house two or three days while my father was showing the films. I was about ten years old and didn't realize that Oscar Micheaux was a famous film maker.

HELEN: When did you find out that he was a famous person?

MISS MASON: After I was grown, when I began to see programs and books in his honor.

HELEN: What did he look like?

MISS MASON: He looked like a 300-pound football player with a dramatic hat and a full-length fur coat. And that was in the days before anybody else was dressing like that.

HELEN: Was he nice?

MISS MASON: Yes, very nice to us children. He would take time and tell us about his adventures.

HELEN: Like what?

MISS MASON: He did all kinds of jobs as a young man. Sometimes he would tell us about how he learned to be a supersalesman

Other times he'd tell us about his experiences working as a shoeshine boy, as a steelworker, or as a rich young rancher in South Dakota. But what I liked best was the train trip he took all through South and Central America.

HELEN: Sounds like his real life was as exciting as a movie!

MISS MASON: It was. My brother and I used to love to sit in the living room and hear him talk, but that wasn't the best memory of all.

HELEN: Then what was?

MISS MASON: Micheaux was a showman. He was more of an actor than any of the stars in his movies. We lived in a little town where nothing much ever happened—until Oscar Micheaux "breezed into town"!

HELEN: Then what happened?

MISS MASON: He'd arrange a big opening night celebration for his new movie. The community center would be decorated. Bands would play. People would get all dressed up. He'd get one of those big Hollywood-type spotlights and then he'd drive up in a big car.

HELEN: That must have been exciting to see him arrive and step into the spotlight.

MISS MASON: Better than that, he let my brother and me ride in the car and be in the spotlight with him!

HELEN: What a thrill! I see why that's the most unforgettable memory of all for you.

(*Children in the class all clap, and one child says, "May I have your autograph, Miss Mason?"*)

MARY MCLEOD BETHUNE

UNLIKE HER PARENTS AND many of her sixteen brothers and sisters, Mary Jane McLeod was born "free." Her birthday was July 10, 1875—ten years after slavery was abolished. Her parents, Samuel and Patsy McLeod, had been slaves near Mayesville, South Carolina. When slavery ended, they remained in that area, but not in slave conditions.

Samuel McLeod was a skillful carpenter and a good farmer. He wanted to establish a lasting home. Mrs. McLeod was a slightly built woman with regal bearing and a strong character. According to family history, her grandmother was the daughter of a chief in Guinea, West Africa.

Like many former slaves, the McLeods became sharecroppers when slavery ended. They did not own any land, but farmed land belonging to a landowner. The landowner would loan them money to buy seed, and for other expenses they had while the crop was growing. When the crop was harvested, they often got only a little bit more money than they had borrowed. Then the next year they would have to borrow more money for seeds and expenses. Even though sharecroppers worked hard, it was almost impossible for them to keep from going into debt.

Mary's parents were determined to better themselves. Mrs. McLeod continued to cook in the home of her former owner, and was paid for her work. She was able to save enough money for the family to buy five acres of land. Thus, the family became landowners. Samuel McLeod and his sons cut logs to build a cabin for the family. Although it was a very simple cabin, the parents made it comfortable.

A deeply religious Methodist family, the McLeods were sometimes visited by traveling ministers. The ministers would hold prayer services out in the yard beneath the big oak tree. Mary enjoyed joining her father in singing hymns and spirituals at these services. The older people, who had known what slavery was like, especially liked to sing "Nobody Knows the Trouble I've Seen." Never having been a slave, Mary could only imagine what it had been like. She learned about it from stories her grandmother and her older brothers and sisters told her.

Many of the old ways of thinking persisted. Once when Mary was very young, she went to work with her mother. She and the daughter of her mother's employer were playing. Mary picked up a book to look at it. Her playmate snatched the book away. She said that since Negroes couldn't read, Mary didn't need a book. That was a turning point in the life of Mary Jane McLeod. She became determined to learn to read.

When Presbyterian missionaries started a school in Mayesville, Mary was anxious to attend. Farming families couldn't manage without putting their children to work in the fields, so the school was just in session for the three months between planting and harvesttime. For four years Mary walked to school—five miles each way. She tried to cram in all the learning she could in the short school year. Her family looked forward to her return each evening. They were eager for her to share what she'd learned that day.

Mary's teacher was a kind, young black woman named Miss Emma Wilson. She read to the children from the Bible and from the writings of Frederick Douglass. Mary wished she could become a teacher just like Miss Wilson, but feared she would not be able to continue her education after she finished the country school. Fortunately, Miss Wilson was able to find a patron for Mary. Just before graduation, Mary learned that Miss Mary Crissmon, a white dressmaker in Colorado, had provided a scholarship. This made it possible for Mary to attend Scotia Seminary in Concord, North Carolina.

Upon graduation from Scotia, Miss Crissmon again provided money to help Mary go on to further study. By this time Mary had decided she wanted to become a missionary. She went to Moody Bible Institute in Chicago. When she was unable to get a placement as a missionary, she went home to teach at the same school she had attended as a child. The following year she took a teaching job at Haines Institute in Augusta, Georgia. Haines was a high school founded by Lucy Laney—in the days when there were few public schools that black students could attend. Lucy Laney was a dynamic role model for Mary McLeod.

From Haines, Mary went to Kimball Institute near her family home in South Carolina. While there, she married a fellow teacher, Albertus Bethune. They had one son, Albert M. Bethune. He was still a baby when Mrs. Bethune was asked to start a mission school in Palatka, Florida. It was successful, but was not what she wanted to do for her life's work. She felt a more pressing need elsewhere in Florida.

The Florida East Coast Railroad was being built at that time. Many black workers and their families were flocking to Florida. Mary Bethune was concerned about these workers and decided that the best thing she could do would be to teach the younger children. She knew from personal experience that this could help whole families. As a child, she had seen her father almost cheated out of money he had earned because he could not count. Mary knew how to count, and because of that her father got the money he was entitled to.

Knowing how important it was to have money to maintain a school, Mary Bethune moved from Palatka to the nearby winter resort town that wealthy northerners visited. In 1904, she went to Daytona Beach. She had $1.50 and plenty of determination. She rented a cottage in the black neighborhood. The landlord trusted her for the rent of the cottage. Her son and five little girls were the only pupils. Things were very difficult at first, but within two years the school had 250 students. Mrs. Bethune, like Lucy Laney before her, encouraged students to develop their minds, hands, and hearts. She believed that the school had a responsibility to the entire community. She organized a hospital when her students were refused service at the local white-operated hospital. She also started a Better Boys Club with activities that attracted boys. Her reasoning was that neighborhood boys needed better things to do than spend time in bars and poolrooms. Many of "her boys" had satisfying and successful lives. One of the best known was Dr. Howard Thurman, who became Professor of Theology at Boston University.

The school outgrew its original location. The only land available to Mary Bethune was the city dump. Not having any money for buildings, she launched a fund-raising campaign. She rode her bicycle down dusty roads, going from house to house pleading for funds. She made speeches and wrote newspaper articles and letters, appealing to wealthy tourists.

Eventually she was able to build Faith Hall where the city dump had been. In order to continue building, pay salaries, and meet the school's other expenses, Mary began traveling around the nation doing fund-raising.

Her school continued to grow. In 1923, it absorbed Cookman Institute, which had been operated by the Methodist Church. The school's new name became Bethune-Cookman College.

Mary McLeod Bethune's success in building a school brought her to national attention. Toward the end of her life she was one of the most influential women in the United States. She served as vice president of the Urban League, president of the Association of Colored Women, and was founder of the National Council of Negro Women. She served as president of the Association for the Study of Negro Life and History. She was an adviser on Negro education to five successive American presidents. She was a friend of Franklin and Eleanor Roosevelt. President Roosevelt's "New Deal" programs were designed to put Americans back to work after the Great Depression. In 1934, Mary Bethune was called to Washington as a special adviser, and in 1936 she was appointed director of the Division of Minority Affairs in the National Youth Administration.

Mrs. Bethune was a special representative of the U.S. State Department at the San Francisco conference that established the United Nations. During World War II, she had worked as special assistant to the Secretary of War for selection of candidates to the Women's Army Corps.

Not surprisingly, Mrs. Bethune received many awards for her work. They included the Spingarn Medal from the National Association for the Advancement of Colored People, the Frances Drexel Award for Distinguished Service, the Thomas Jefferson Award for outstanding leadership. She also received the Medal of Honor and Merit from the Republic of Haiti, and the Star of Africa from the Republic of Liberia, as well as many honorary degrees.

On May 18, 1955, just before her eightieth birthday, Mary McLeod Bethune died of a heart attack. Since Mrs. Bethune's death, her work has been honored in many ways. Two of the most notable are in Washington, D.C. One is a statue in Lincoln Park, and the other is the Mary McLeod Bethune Museum and Archives, a National Historic Site designated by an act of Congress. She is buried on the campus of Bethune-Cookman College, the school she built. Her eulogy was delivered by Dr. Howard Thurman, her former pupil.

Let Them Have Schools

๛

CAST

Mary McLeod Bethune
First Narrator
Second Narrator

MARY MCLEOD BETHUNE: (*counting change*) $1.25, $1.35, $1.45, $1.46, $1.47, $1.48, $1.49, $1.50. Just one dollar and fifty cents. I'm glad the landlord will trust me for the rent on this little cottage. I do hope I can get a school started here. Our people have such a *need* for education.

FIRST NARRATOR: On October 4, 1904, Mary McLeod Bethune opened her school in Daytona Beach, Florida, with her son and five little girls whose parents paid fifty cents a week. They skimped along.

MARY MCLEOD BETHUNE: We burned logs, then used the charred splints as pencils, and washed elderberries for our ink.

SECOND NARRATOR: Orange crates served as benches, and Mrs. Bethune haunted the city dump for discarded items she could recycle for her school.

MARY MCLEOD BETHUNE: In less than two years, we had 250 pupils.

FIRST NARRATOR: And it continued to grow. Eventually the school became Bethune-Cookman College and was known around the world.

SECOND NARRATOR: How did Mrs. Bethune get interested in teaching?

FIRST NARRATOR: An early chilldhood experience made Mary realize how reading could liberate black people. She became *determined* to learn and to teach.

SECOND NARRATOR: She grew up at a time when it was almost impossible for a black child to get an education.

FIRST NARRATOR: Mary was the youngest of seventeen children born to former slaves. She felt lucky to have a school just five miles away. Mary walked to school everyday, then she'd come home and teach her family what she'd learned.

MARY MCLEOD BETHUNE: A whole world opened up when I learned to read!

SECOND NARRATOR: Is that what made her want to become a teacher?

FIRST NARRATOR: Well, her first dream was to become a missionary in Africa. But she wasn't able to do that after all.

SECOND NARRATOR: What did she do then?

FIRST NARRATOR: Well, first she went to Haines Institute in Georgia. It was a school founded by a black woman named Lucy Craft Laney.

SECOND NARRATOR: Did Mrs. Bethune go to Florida from there?

FIRST NARRATOR: No, she went to Sumpter, South Carolina. She met Mr. Albertus Bethune, who was also a teacher.

SECOND NARRATOR: So that's how she got to be Mary McLeod Bethune! Did the Bethunes stay in South Carolina?

FIRST NARRATOR: No, they moved to Savannah, Georgia. Their son was born during the two years they lived there.

SECOND NARRATOR: (*exasperated*) Well, how did they get to Florida? That's what I want to know.

FIRST NARRATOR: They moved there and Mr. Bethune died soon after they arrived.

SECOND NARRATOR: What did Mrs. Bethune do then?

FIRST NARRATOR: A Mr. Flagler was building a railroad and hundreds of black men had gone there to do construction work. Most of these workers could neither read nor write. Neither could their children.

SECOND NARRATOR: I thought you said that Mrs. Bethune started a school with her son and five little girls.

FIRST NARRATOR: I did. Mrs. Bethune felt that girls were especially hampered by the lack of educational opportunities.

SECOND NARRATOR: I know Mrs. Bethune's work didn't stop with her school. She helped organize the National Association of Colored Women's Clubs and the National Council of Negro Women. She was special adviser on minority affairs to President Franklin D. Roosevelt during the Depression, and was awarded the NAACP's Spingarn Medal and many honorary degrees.

FIRST NARRATOR: She was not only a great educator, she was a great woman.

SECOND NARRATOR: Learning to read really *did* open up some whole new worlds for her and for a lot of other people, too!

FIRST NARRATOR: Mrs. Bethune's mother was of royal African blood. In Mary McLeod Bethune's own words:

MARY MCLEOD BETHUNE: I am my mother's daughter, and the drums of Africa still beat in my heart. They will not let me rest while there is a single Negro boy or girl without a chance to prove his worth.

LEROY "SATCHEL" PAIGE

THE LEGENDARY BASEBALL PITCHER, Leroy "Satchel" Paige, used to say, "I started out as a pitcher." For practice, "I tossed stones at tin cans all day long." Paige's after-school jobs gave him even more of a chance to develop his arm. One job was delivering large blocks of ice. The other was carrying baggage at Union Station in his hometown of Mobile, Alabama. Some say he got the nickname "Satchel" because the bags were called "satchels." Others say that the name referred to his big "satchel-sized" feet.

Nobody ever knew Paige's exact age. Most biographers say he was born on July 7, 1906. Other writers claim he was born in 1904. The record books say he retired at fifty-nine, but he may have been sixty-one or even sixty-nine. There is agreement on the fact that his parents were John and Lula Paige and that he was born in Mobile, one of a large family of children.

Like many things about Paige's life, the exact time and place of his professional debut are not known. What is known is that "Satchel" Paige was one of the most brilliant pitchers that ever lived. He progressed from sandlot, to semi-pro, to profes-

sional baseball. In the mid-1920s, he played for teams in the all-Negro Southern Association—the Mobile Tigers, the Black Lookouts of Chattanooga, the Birmingham Black Barons, the Nashville Elite Giants, and the New Orleans Black Pelicans. In the 1930s, he played in South America and the Caribbean during the winter. In the summer he played in western United States—in Denver, Colorado, and Bismarck, North Dakota. He became the first black player in the American League as the Cleveland Indians made their run for the pennant in 1948.

Paige commanded one of the highest salaries in baseball in his day. Yet he started out very humbly. His first "paying" job was in 1924. The Mobile Tigers—the first semi-pro team he played for—used to pass the hat among the spectators. If the collection was good, Paige was paid $1.00 per game. Otherwise he was given a keg of lemonade as payment for pitching a game. His first real paying job was with the Black Lookouts of Chattanooga for $50 a month. After that, he was with various black baseball teams, always as pitcher and oftentimes as the star attraction for the team. He joined the Kansas City Monarchs in 1942. With his pitching, the team won the Negro American League pennant that year and again in 1946 when Paige allowed only two runs in 93 innings.

Paige was a real showman, and appreciative black fans came out in large numbers. Sportswriters for the black press kept their readers well informed, but many other Americans had little knowledge about the teams and players in the Negro leagues. There was little coverage in the big city daily papers, and television was just coming into existence.

American society and major league baseball were not yet

integrated. Black organized baseball and white organized base-ball operated in two separate worlds. Black teams had to ride segregated buses and trains or crowd nine men into a car and drive to out-of-town games. The players kept their spirits up by singing as they rode. Paige provided accompaniment with his guitar. Frequently after traveling long distances, the teams had a hard time finding lodging. In small towns the players had to stay at private homes or local boarding houses, for white-owned hotels would not accept them. Sometimes they had to sleep on the bus or in dugouts at the ball park. At other times they'd ride all night and arrive in town just in time for the game. It was equally hard to find eating places. Paige used to refuse to pitch in any town where he could not find a place to stay or eat. In the larger cities, players could find lodging and food at some of the better black hotels and restaurants. In spite of the inconveniences caused by racial segregation, the Negro leagues produced some very fine players—such as eventual Hall of Fame members Josh Gibson, "Cool Papa" Bell, Oscar Charleston, Judy Johnson, and "Satchel" Paige, of course.

Even though they operated separately, the Negro leagues and major leagues met each other in exhibition games. Both black and white sportswriters publicized pitching duels be-tween such greats as "Satchel" Paige and Dizzy Dean or Bob Feller. Paige's pitching earned the respect of outstanding ath-letes. Dizzy Dean said he'd seen the finest pitchers, and "Paige is the best." Joe DiMaggio called Paige "the fastest pitcher I've ever faced."

Paige's remarkable career spanned portions of five decades.

He played from the mid-1920s to the late 1960s. He is credited with having played about 2,500 games and winning 2,000 of them. He pitched 300 shutouts and 55 no-hitters. In 1933 he pitched 31 games and lost only 4. In 1934, when he was in North Dakota, he pitched 29 consecutive games and won 28. He pitched in every game that season. His record was 105 games played, 104 won. Other records include a winning streak of 21 consecutive wins, 64 scoreless innings, and 22 strikeouts in one game.

Paige was often booked as a solo star. He'd pitch for any team that would meet his price, reportedly $500 to $2,000 a game, and would guarantee "9 strikeouts in 3 innings." The Baltimore Black Sox, the Pittsburgh Crawfords, the Newark Eagles, the Homestead (Pennsylvania) Grays, and the Chicago American Giants are some of the teams he pitched for or appeared with at various times.

In 1948, Bill Veeck was president of the Cleveland Indians. Cleveland was fighting to win the American League pennant. It was the year after the Brooklyn Dodgers had hired Jackie Robinson and removed the color bar in the National League. Veeck had seen Paige pitch and thought he was what Cleveland needed, so he signed him. Paige won six games and lost only one. Cleveland cinched the pennant and went on to win the World Series.

Although Paige was past his prime by the time he had an opportunity to play in the major leagues, he could still attract large crowds. He brought in 200,000 fans in three games at Cleveland. In 1951 he moved to the St. Louis Browns and was their most valuable pitcher through the 1953 season. A high point of his stint there was when Casey Stengel chose Paige as a pitcher on the 1952 American League All-Star team. Paige was greatly disappointed when the game was halted by rain prior to his appearance on the mound.

Paige officially retired from the Browns at the end of the 1953 season. Having entered the major leagues late in his career, he held the distinction of being the oldest "rookie." When he retired, he was the oldest player ever to play in a major league game. Although retired from league play, Paige continued to pitch exhibition games and delight the fans. He spent off-seasons at home in Kansas City with his wife, Lahoma, and their children. He became active in politics. In 1968 he

made an unsuccessful run for the Missouri legislature. That same year the Atlanta Braves signed him as a coach to make him eligible for a major league pension.

Paige was one of the first players to be enshrined when the National Baseball Hall of Fame was opened to stars in the Negro leagues. At his induction, he said, "I'm the proudest man on the face of the earth today."

"Satchel" Paige died in June of 1982, suffering from emphysema and heart disease. Just three days before, he was the star attraction in a ball park when a stadium in the heart of Kansas City's black community was renamed the "Satchel" Paige Stadium. It was a fitting tribute to the ageless man who was one of the greatest pitchers of all time.

The Rediscovery of "Satchel" Paige

꙳

CAST

Daddy   Son
Daughter   Grandpa

SCENE I

The family is cleaning the attic.

DAUGHTER: Daddy, what's in this trunk?

DADDY: Oh, that has all my old treasures in it.

SON: You mean silver and gold?

DADDY: No, I never had silver or gold, Son. They are my personal treasures—the things that were special to me as I was growing up.

DAUGHTER: Like what, Daddy?

DADDY: Oh, certificates, badges, baseball cards—things like that.

SON: Baseball cards? Did they have baseball cards way back when you were a kid?

DADDY: (*chuckling as he speaks*) Yes, they had them when I was a kid. If I remember correctly, I put them on top of everything else.

DAUGHTER: Can we see?

DADDY: Sure. It will be kind of fun for me, too.

SON: Did any of the modern players start back in your day?

DADDY: (*raising trunk lid and sorting through cards until he finds the one he wants*) No, but here's the picture of a man who played longer than anyone else I ever heard of.

DAUGHTER: Who is it?

DADDY: (*looking at the baseball card in his hand*) This is "Satchel" Paige.

SON: "Satchel"?

DAUGHTER: I never heard of anybody with that name before.

SON: Was that his real name?

DADDY: No, his real name was Leroy Robert Paige, but everybody called him "Satchel."

DAUGHTER: Why?

DADDY: Some folks said because he used to carry so many suit-cases—or satchels—at once when he worked as a porter in the train station. Others say it was because he had such big feet. I don't know why he had that nickname, but I do know he probably pitched and won more games than anybody else in baseball history. He was a pitching genius.

SON: Did you ever see him pitch?

DADDY: Yes. When I was about six years old, my daddy—your grandpa—took me out to see old "Satchel" pitch in an exhibition game. He was long past his prime, but he was still exciting to watch.

DAUGHTER: What was he like?

DADDY: Well, he was tall—six feet, four inches. (*looking at the back of the baseball card in his hand*) Although this card says he weighed 190 pounds, he looked like a lanky kid, even though he must have been in his sixties by that time.

SON: Wow, he *was* old to be playing baseball!

DADDY: (*remembering the day he saw "Satchel" Paige pitch*) Yes, but he wasn't too old to put on a show. The crowd loved him!

DAUGHTER: What did he do?

DADDY: For one thing he'd stroll to the mound like he had never had a worry in the world, then he'd wind up, stick out his big foot and do one of his "hesitation" pitches. It was like watching a pitch in slow motion. Your grandpa is the one who can really tell you about Paige. Ask him at supper tonight.

SCENE II

Everyone's sitting around the supper table.

DAUGHTER: Grandpa, Daddy started telling us about "Satchel" Paige today, but he said you were the one who really knew about him as a pitcher.

GRANDPA: Yes, I'm enough older than your daddy that I really got to see the man in action. He could almost twist himself into a pretzel, and by the time the batter knew what had happened, the umpire was calling "STRIKE!" In his heyday, Paige could pitch so fast it was just a blur. He had one ball he'd throw so fast it would hum. He called that one "the bee ball."

DAUGHTER: Where did you see him play, Grandpa?

GRANDPA: In Kansas City—when he was with the Monarchs. Jackie Robinson had played for them, too, you know.

SON: (who has done a little reading during the day) No, I didn't know that. I did know that Robinson was the first black person to play in the major leagues.

GRANDPA: Branch Rickey hired Jackie Robinson and Bill Veeck hired Larry Doby and "Satchel" Paige. They let the rest of the nation see some of the great players we'd been watching in the Negro leagues. It's just too bad that Paige didn't get a chance to go to the major leagues before he was in his forties.

SON: Wow, he must have been something! Daddy said "Satchel" was about sixty when he saw him. Most modern players stop playing by the time they're forty.

DADDY: Back then most players retired by forty, too.

GRANDPA: Paige was just exceptional. When he got so that he couldn't throw that fast ball anymore, he developed an incredible assortment of pitches. Batters never knew what was coming—and his control was fantastic. I can picture him now, laughing and talking all through the game. He was a man who loved baseball and life.

DADDY: See, kids, I told you Grandpa could tell you about "old Satch."

DAUGHTER: He sure did.

SON: Daddy, I'm glad you opened your treasure trunk this morning.

DADDY: You know, I am too. (*looking at his watch*) Say, we got to talking and it's way past your bedtime. Time to say "goodnight."

DAUGHTER: Aw, do we *have* to go now?

DADDY: Yes, it's pretty late.

SON: Grandpa, can you tell us just one more thing about "Satchel" Paige?

GRANDPA: All right, one more thing. You've seen baseball players wearing helmets, haven't you? A teammate who used to play with "Satchel" said that it was because of him. An opposing team was so afraid of his fast balls that they protected their heads with helmets, and the idea caught on.

SON: Wow, that's something!

DAUGHTER: Good-night, Daddy.

SON: Good-night, Grandpa.

MAGGIE LENA WALKER

MAGGIE LENA WALKER had 15,000 "grandchildren." These were not actually her grandchildren, but children who were enrolled in the thrift clubs sponsored by the St. Luke Order, which Maggie Walker headed. The children were taught how to bank and save money. Each was given a "rainy day" bank of cardboard. When he or she had saved a whole dollar, from doing chores or other work, the group leader encouraged the youngster to put the dollar in a regular savings bank. Many of the children had savings of $100 to $400.

Maggie Walker used to tell children that small savings would grow into big savings. She personally reached many school-children with this message in Richmond, Virginia, where she had established the Penny Savings Bank. Other thousands knew of Maggie as the "St. Luke Grandmother" in the children's page of the *St. Luke Herald* newspaper. That page was special to them because it featured pictures of them and their letters, as well as riddles, stories, and articles about saving money.

Maggie Lena Walker edited the children's page and all the other pages of the *St. Luke Herald*. She also became the very

first woman in the United States to found a bank and become its president.

Anyone who had seen Maggie grow up wouldn't have been at all surprised at her accomplishments. She had always been a person who knew exactly what she wanted to achieve and how to do it. Born in Richmond on July 15, 1867—just two years after the end of the Civil War—Maggie grew up at a time when career opportunities for women, especially black women, were very limited. She didn't let that discourage her, though. If opportunities didn't exist, she would have to create them. She knew what hard work was all about. Maggie's widowed mother washed clothes for wealthy people in order to support Maggie and her little brother, John. Maggie had to help.

As a schoolgirl, Maggie was the best math student in Lancaster School. She finished Richmond Normal and Colored School just before she turned sixteen, and was qualified as a teacher. But she preferred to do bookkeeping and only men could get jobs as bookkeepers. Maggie decided to do something about that.

The Order of St. Luke was a black fraternal and cooperative insurance venture. It was founded in Baltimore, Maryland, by an ex-slave woman named Mary Prout. Members paid weekly dues, and were given financial help when they needed it. Maggie's mother belonged to the Order, and on Maggie's fourteenth birthday she also joined. When she wanted a job as a bookkeeper, she decided to apply to St. Luke's. But the man she talked with only suggested that she get some business experience and come back later.

She took a job as a teacher and taught until her marriage to Armistead Walker, whose family was in the construction business. Maggie became a homemaker and mother. The Walkers had two sons, Russell and Melvin.

Her interest in the St. Luke Order continued and she became an organizer for the group. In 1895, she suggested that St. Luke form a juvenile branch and she drew up the rules for governing the Juvenile Circles. She assumed more and more responsibilities, and in 1899 Maggie Walker became Grand Secretary Treasurer of the entire organization. This was quite an accomplishment for a woman who had been denied a job as a bookkeeper. St. Luke's was in financial trouble when Maggie took over, but she soon had it growing and prospering.

In 1902, Maggie Walker proposed the establishment of the St. Luke Penny Savings Bank. She became its president—America's first woman bank president. Later the bank's name was changed to the St. Luke Bank and Trust Company and became the bank for Richmond city taxes and gas and water accounts. Still later, it merged with two other banks, and to this day it continues as the Consolidated Bank and Trust Company.

Under Maggie's leadership, the Order of St. Luke continued to grow. She could be very persuasive. By 1927 there were branches in twenty-two states, and hundreds of members were helped to start their own businesses. The bank provided loans and mortgages, and Maggie always insisted on the importance of saving. She was happiest over the fact that 15,000 children were enrolled in the thrift clubs.

Maggie Lena Walker also found time for other community

activities. She was president of the Richmond club of the National Federation of Colored Women's Clubs, and helped raise funds for needed facilities for blacks. She received many honors. In 1924, the citizens of Richmond paid tribute to her, and the governor of the state was present. She received an honorary degree from Virginia Union University. A theater, a street, and a school have been named for her.

Maggie Lena Walker died in 1934. Following a fall in 1907, she had been confined to a wheelchair. Today her home in Richmond, Virginia, is a National Historic Site, and the National Park Service maintains it, so that the American public can visit it.

Miracles Do Happen!

⁊◐

CAST

Davy, a lame shoeshine boy
  who saves what he earns
Billy and Jimmy, two other
  shoeshine boys who
  spend their money and
  tease Davy

Narrator
Maggie Lena Walker

SCENE 1

NARRATOR: This scene takes place in the area around Second and Clay streets in Richmond, Virginia, one afternoon in the early 1900s. All three boys are walking home after work.

BILLY and JIMMY: (*calling to Davy while they munch on candy bars*) Stingy! Stingy! Stingy!

JIMMY: Davy, you sure are dumb not to buy yourself some candy after work.

BILLY: Yeah. "All work and no play makes Davy a dull boy."

DAVY: (*with tears in his eyes*) Sometimes I buy one.

NARRATOR: It really hurt Davy's feelings when the other boys called him "stingy," but he couldn't explain just then, so he took their teasing.

SCENE 2

NARRATOR: One morning a few days later, the boys meet at their usual meeting place. Davy doesn't have his shoeshine box, but seems really happy about something.

BILLY: Where's your box, Davy?

DAVY: Follow me.

NARRATOR: Billy and Jimmy looked at each other, wondering what Davy meant. They followed him down the street until they got to a little shop. Billy and Jimmy peered in the window. Inside there stood three nice chairs for customers to sit in when they came to get their shoes shined.

JIMMY: Wow! I never noticed this shop before.

BILLY: Whose shop is this?

NARRATOR: Instead of saying anything, Davy reached in his pocket, took out a key, and opened the door to the shop. The two boys were amazed.

JIMMY: Is this really your place, Davy?

DAVY: Yeah.

BILLY: Where . . . I mean . . . how'd ya get it?

DAVY: From the bank president.

JIMMY: Yeah. Sure. Davy, I can't believe that. Nobody is giving anything away!

DAVY: No, really. Mrs. Walker will help any person who shows that he can be thrifty.

BILLY: Mrs. Walker? Who ever heard of a woman bank president?

DAVY: She's not only the bank president. If you join the St. Luke Order and save $50, she'll help you, too. She helped me rent this place.

SCENE 3

NARRATOR: Seven years later in the bank. A well-dressed young man asks Mrs. Walker's secretary if he may speak with Mrs. Walker. The young man is lame.

DAVY: (*to Mrs. Walker*) Hello, Mrs. Walker. My name is Davy. You may not remember me, but seven years ago you helped me rent a little shoeshine shop.

MRS. WALKER: Hello, Davy. I remember you very well. How are you? Are you still in the shoeshine business?

DAVY: Yes, ma'am. Things are going well. Now I own my own place with twelve customer chairs, and I was able to buy a home for my mother.

MRS. WALKER: How wonderful! I'm certainly glad to hear that. It sounds like you're continuing your habit of saving.

DAVY: Yes, ma'am. I paid $1,900 for my mother's house, and I have furnished it. Even so, I don't owe anybody a dime. I am free of debt and never let my bank account get below $500.

MRS. WALKER: Yours is the kind of success story I love to hear.

DAVY: Well, I think you deserve the credit for getting kids to save. That sure made a big difference in my life, and I just wanted to come say "Thank you" again.

Index

Abernathy, Ralph, 16, 29, 34
Abolitionists, 107
Acosta, José Julian, 36
Addams, Jane, 120
Air Force, U.S., 84, 85
Anderson, Marian, 49
Anti-Slavery Society, 107
Association for the Study of Negro
    Life and History, 143
Association of Colored Women, 143
Atlanta, Georgia, 13, 15, 17
Attucks, Crispus, 119
Auld, Mrs. Sophia, 106

Baerga, Flor, 38
Bailey, Frederick. *See* Douglass, Fred-
    erick
Banneker, Benjamin, 119
Barber, Samuel, 53
Barnett, Alfreda, 120
Barnett, Charles, 120
Barnett, Ferdinand Lee, 119–120
Barnett, Herman, 120
Barnett, Ida, 120
Beattie, John, Dr., 94, 95
"Beauty of Being Free, The" (skit),
    122–127
Bell, "Cool Papa," 152
Bethune, Albertus, 142
Bethune, Mary McLeod, 9, 139–148
    skit about, 145–148

Bethune-Cookman College, 143,
    144
Brau, Salvador, 36
Brown, John, 108
Bruce, John E., 39
Carnegie, Andrew, 73
Carnegie Corporation, 39, 40
Carnegie Hero Fund Commission,
    73
Cattlett, Alice Elizabeth. *See* White,
    Mrs. Charles (Alice)
Charleston, Oscar, 152
Chicago Public Library, 61
Chisholm family, 51
Civil rights, 13, 19, 25
Civil rights movement, 25, 30, 34
Civil War, 109
Civilian Aeronautics Administration,
    84
Congress for Racial Equality, 17
Crissmon, Mary, 141

Davis, Benjamin O., Jr. 84, 86
Dean, Dizzy, 152
Desegregation, 30, 34
DiMaggio, Joe, 152
Discrimination, 17, 96, 108
Douglass, Frederick, 9, 105–114, 141
    skit about, 110–114
Douglass, Mrs. Frederick (Anna),
    107, 110–114

"Douglass 'Station' of the Underground Railroad, The" (skit), 110–114
Drew, Charles, 10, 92–103
  skit about, 98–103
Drew, Lenore, 95
Drew, Nora, 92
Drew, Richard, 92

"Eagles Return to the Nest, The" (skit), 88–91
Ebenezer Baptist Church, 13, 17
Emancipation Proclamation, 109
Equal rights, 25
Evers, Medgar, 18

Farrell, Thomas A., 73
Feller, Bob, 152
Fifteenth Amendment, 117
Fortune, T. Thomas, 119
"Freedom Riders," 17

Gandhi, Mahatma, 17
General Electric Company, 75
Gershwin, Ira, 52
Gibson, Josh, 152

Harlem Renaissance, 39
Hassek, Mary Anne. *See* Morgan, Mrs. Garrett A. (Mary)
Homer, Winslow, 60

"In the Footsteps of Dr. King" (skit), 20–24
Integration, 17–18
International Exposition for Sanitation and Safety, 71

James, Charles, 83
James, Claude, 86
James, Danice, 86
James, Daniel, 86
James, Daniel, Sr., 82
James, Daniel "Chappie," 10, 81–91
  skit about, 88–91

James, Mrs. Daniel (Dorothy), 83, 86
"Jim Crow" laws, 13–14, 17, 28, 29
Johnson, George, 130, 131
Johnson, Judy, 152
Joseph, Mary. *See* Schomburg, Mrs. Charles
Joseph, Nicholas, 36
Julius Rosenwald Foundation, 61
Justice, 13, 118

Kelsey, George, 15
Kimball, Florence Page, 51
King, Alberta Williams, 13, 14
King, Alfred Daniel, 13
King, Christine, 13
King, Martin Luther, Jr., 9, 13–24, 28, 29, 30, 34
  skit about, 20–24
King, Martin Luther, 13, 14, 16, 17
King, Mrs. Martin Luther, Jr. (Coretta), 16, 17, 29
King, Yolanda, 16
Korean War, 85

Laney, Lucy, 141, 142
"Legacy of Dignity and Pride, A" (skit), 42–48
"Let Them Have Schools" (skit), 145–148
Lincoln, Abraham, 109
Lincoln Motion Picture Company, 131
Locke, Alain, 39, 60
London, Jack, 131
Luther, Martin, 13
Lynching, 119

Mays, Benjamin E., Dr., 15
McKenna, Hattie V.J., 49
McLeod, Mary Jane. *See* Bethune, Mary McLeod
McLeod, Patsy, 139–140
McLeod, Samuel, 139–140
"Meet the Inventor of the Stoplight" (skit), 76–79

Micheaux, Belle, 130
Micheaux, Calvin, 130
Micheaux, Oscar, 10, 129–137
  skit about, 134–137
"Miracles Do Happen!" (skit), 166–169
Montgomery, Alabama, 16, 17, 25, 29–30
Morgan, Elizabeth Reed, 69
Morgan, Frank, 72
Morgan, Garrett A., 10, 69–79
  skit about, 76–79
Morgan, Mrs. Garrett A. (Mary), 69, 71
Morgan, Sydney, 69

National Association for the Advancement of Colored People (NAACP), 26, 28, 33, 53, 84, 96, 120, 144
National Council of Negro Women, 143
National Council of Women, 109
National Safety Device Company, 72
National Urban League, 39, 143
National Youth Administration, 144
Negro Society for Historical Research, 39
New Negro, The (Locke), 39, 60
New York Public Library, 39, 40
Nixon, E. D., 28–29, 33–34
North American Air Defense Command (NORAD), 86

Order of St. Luke, 161, 163, 164
"Oscar Micheaux's Visit" (skit), 134–137

Paige, John, 149
Paige, Lahoma, 154
Paige, Leroy "Satchel," 10, 149–160
  skit about, 157–160
Paige, Lula, 149

Pareja, Juan de, 38
Parks, Raymond A., 25
Parks, Rosa, 9, 16, 25–34
  skit about, 31–34
Poor People's March on Washington, 18
Prejudice, 14, 60, 72, 73, 107, 108
Price, George, 49
Price, Leontyne, 9, 49–57
  skit about, 54–57
"Priceless Leontyne, The" (skit), 54–57
Prout, Mary, 163

Racism, 73
Ray, James Earl, 19
"Rediscovery of 'Satchel' Paige, The" (skit), 156–160
Robeson, Paul, 51, 133
Robinson, Jackie, 153
Roosevelt, Eleanor, 143
Roosevelt, Franklin, 143
Rosenwald Foundation, 61
Ruggles, David, 107

St. Luke Order, 161, 163, 164
Schomburg, Arthur A., 9, 35–48
  skit about, 42–48
Schomburg, Charles, 36
Schomburg, Mrs. Arthur, 40
Schomburg, Mrs. Charles, 36
Schomburg Center for Research in Black Culture, 40
Scott, Coretta. *See* King, Mrs. Martin Luther, Jr.
Segregation, 14, 16, 17, 25, 29, 152
Sharecroppers, 139–140
Slavery, 41, 107–108, 115, 139, 140
Southern Christian Leadership Conference (SCLC), 17
Spingarn Medal, 53, 96, 144
Stengel, Casey, 154
Student Nonviolent Coordinating Committee, 17
Supreme Court, U.S., 17, 29

Terrell, Mary Church, 120
Thompson, Virgil, 52
Thurman, Howard, Dr., 143, 144
"Turning Point in the Life of Charles White, A" (skit), 63–68
Tuskegee Institute, 83, 84

"Unexpected Heroine, The" (skit), 31–34
United Nations, 144

Veeck, Bill, 153
Verdi, 52
Voters League, 26

Walker, Armistead, 164
Walker, Maggie Lena, 10, 161–169
  skit about, 166–169
Walker, Melvin, 164
Walker, Russell, 164

Wallace, George, 17
Warfield, William, 52
Watkins, Dorothy. *See* James, Mrs. Daniel (Dorothy)
Wells, Elizabeth, 115, 117
Wells, Ida B., 9, 115–127
  skit about, 122–127
Wells, James, 115, 117, 122–127
White, Charles, 10, 59–68
  skit about, 63–68
White, Ethel Gary, 59, 62
White, Mrs. Charles (Alice), 61
"Who Was Dr. Charles Drew?" (skit), 98–103
Wilson, Emma, 141
Women's Army Corps, 144
Women's Loyal League, 119
Women's rights, 109, 121
Woods, Granville, 119
Works Progress Administration, 61

GLENNETTE TILLEY TURNER, a teacher for nearly twenty-five years, has firsthand knowledge of how children love to participate actively in learning. She knows that youngsters enjoy reading about real people and presenting skits. As a child in North Carolina, and later in Florida and Illinois, she herself was intrigued with the way people met challenges, and especially liked reading biographies.

She was named Outstanding Woman Educator in DuPage County, Illinois, where she lives with her husband. Recently retired, she now devotes most of her time to writing. She is the author of *Surprise for Mrs. Burns, The Underground Railroad in DuPage County, Illinois,* a biography of Lewis Latimer, and numerous articles in such publications as *Scholastic Scope, Ebony, Jr!,* the *Chicago Tribune, Encore,* and *Elancée* magazines. Glennette Tilley Turner is a former president of the Black Literary Umbrella and the Children's Reading Roundtable of Chicago.

ELTON C. FAX has illustrated numerous books, including his own *Through Black Eyes: Journeys of a Black Artist to East Africa and Russia* and *West Africa Vignettes.* He is the author of *Contemporary Black Leaders, Seventeen Black Artists,* and *Garvey.* Born in Baltimore, Maryland, he received a BFA degree from Syracuse University. He lives in Woodside, New York.